Among the many who ma
West in the fab...
was one Ma...
horse-th...

flight legal counsel, research workers, and investigators. The strange story the authors have pieced together from the evidence uncovered and the legal rebuffs encountered adds up to one of the most intriguing episodes in American history . . . and one that promises loud repercussions today.

The Author

Estelle Cothran Latta was born and reared in North Carolina and educated at the University of North Carolina and Duke University. She is a descendant, on her father's side, of Mark Hopkins' brother James, and on her mother's side of Mark Hopkins' brother Martin. From her early childhood she was intrigued by the story of the migration of Mark and Moses Hopkins and was deeply interested in learning further details of her famous ancestor. However, it was not until she was a graduate student of history at the University of North Carolina that she found the opportunity to delve into the peculiar circumstances surrounding the death of Hopkins and the fraudulent distribution of his fortune. Since then, working with the support of the rightful heirs to the estate, Mrs. Latta has devoted more than twenty years to unearthing the true identity and life story of Mark Hopkins.

(Jack Williams, Durham, N. C.)

Estelle Latta, a double grand-niece of Mark Hopkins.

Mark Hopkins . . . twenty-two years of age. This
was the tintype picture reproduced by the California
Historical Society . . . and now on record in their
department as the true and authentic picture of Mark
Hopkins . . . from Randolph County, North Carolina
. . . son of Edward Hopkins and Hannah Crow Hopkins . . . who later became the Great Railroad Magnate and Empire Builder.

Mark Hopkins of North Carolina

Controversial
Mark Hopkins

by ESTELLE LATTA

in collaboration with Mary L. Allison

SECOND EDITION

REVISED EDITION

Publisher
COTHRAN HISTORICAL AND RESEARCH FOUNDATION
430 - 22nd Street, Sacramento, California
Duke University, Durham, North Carolina

TRUE IDENTITY OF MARK HOPKINS, THE GREAT RAILROAD MAGNATE

The Judgment of the Adjudicated Heirship of Mark Hopkins is suffice to claim his true identity throughout the civilized world. The places in which he held great eminence and world renown recognition during his span of the few short years in which he emassed one of the most fabulous estates known to history, civilization, or characterized by relative progress in the arts, science, and advancement of social culture and the entire economical structure of the United States of America.

The "Heirship" recordation began around two years ago. The treasured "INSTRUMENT"—and "DOCUMENT" lay dormant for years in San Francisco. It was subpoenaed in Judge Hoyt's Court, by Busick & Busick Law Firm, defendant "COUNSEL" for Estelle Latta et al, and at the request of Estelle Latta as their "PLAINTIFF"—.

The "Heirship" was presented which I held the copy of as a compliment from Judge and Doctor Longden—and to whom they gave full credulence to my Father, William Anderson Cothran, and Mother, Susan Ann Vaughan Cothran, for having supplied the documental data which were the fundamental basis upon which the cause of action was incepted and designed.

However, Judge Hoyt (knowing the controversies involved) demanded my defendant counsel bring in the "Heirship Document" as I had on my copy that it was properly recorded in Department No. 9—in San Francisco. He wanted the "Copy" as it appeared in this Department—and certified to by the Clerk of the Court, et cetera. His request was complied, with reference to the subpoena. However, it took a long period of waiting for an impatient court (a day and a half)—to even locate the document.

When it was finally brought into the court room the file recordation showed: "IT WAS IN THE INVENTORY AND BOND PAPERS OF MARY FRANCES SHERWOOD HOPKINS, AND THE SAMUEL FREDERICK HOPKINS LINEAGE!" However, there was no discrepancy in the "Document" that I introduced than the one brought in from "The Clerk's Office in San Francisco!"—The significance of the filing herein referred to was this: Apparently, the entire lineage of Lockport, New York Hopkins's had been using the treasured "JUDGEMENT" for personal conveyances: There were many names in "DEEDS OF CONVEYANCES ET CETERA, ET CETERA, WHICH BORE THE NAMES OF THE TRUE AND LAWFUL HEIRS OF THE RAILROAD MAGNATE—OF Bedding County, Virginia, and North Carolina!"

Shortly thereafter the trial as above referred to: "ESTELLE LATTA BEGAN RECORDATION OF HEIRSHIP THROUGHOUT THE STATE OF CALIFORNIA!" It is now recorded in fifty-five Counties of the fifty-eight counties of the length and breadth in the State of California.

The three which have refused the recordation will soon be served with a mandamus. This would compel them to meet the legal requirements for the constructive notice that Mark Hopkins died, seized and possessed the Real and Personal property of record in each respective County throughout the State of California.

HEIRSHIP JUDGMENT

NORTH CAROLINA,
RANDOLPH COUNTY,

IN THE SUPERIOR COURT

Sandy Young Hopkins, Laura Hopkins
Kirk, Norman Lee Freeman and   } JUDGMENT
Blanche Freeman, et als.,

-vs.-

W. L. Hill

****

This cause coming on to be heard at October Term, 1931, 1 of Superior Court of Randolph County before His Honor, N. A. Sinclair, Judge, and a jury, and the jury having answered the issues submitted to them as follows:

1. Were James Hopkins, John Hopkins, Joseph Hopkins, Martin Hopkins, Elizabeth Hopkins, Prudence Hopkins, Annie Hopkins, Moses Hopkins, Mark Hopkins and Rebecca Hopkins the children, heirs-at-law and next of kin of Edward Hopkins and Hannah Crow Hopkins of Crow Creek, New Hope Township, Randolph County, North Carolina.

Answer: Yes.

2. If so, was Mark Hopkins, son of Edward and Hannah Crow Hopkins the same person who went to California and became Treasurer of the Central Railroad and an organizer of the Ione Coal and Iron Company?

Answer: Yes.

3. Are the plaintiffs in this action the heirs-at-law and next of kin of the said Edward Hopkins, Hannah Crow Hopkins, Mark and Moses Hopkins?

Answer: Yes.

4. Are the plaintiffs the owner of the land described in the complaint?

Answer: No.

IT IS THEREFORE considered and adjudged that the plaintiffs are the sole heirs-at-law of Edward Hopkins and Hannah Crow Hopkins, and of Mark Hopkins and Moses Hopkins, but that the plaintiffs are not the owners of the land described in the complaint, the same being to the defendant, W. L. Hill. It is further adjudged that the plaintiffs pay the cost of the action, to be taxed by the clerk.

N. A. Sinclair
JUDGE PRESIDING

NORTH CAROLINA
Randolph County

I, Maude Lee Boling, Ass't. Clerk Superior Court of said County and State, do hereby certify the attached sheets to be and contain a true and correct copy of the complaint, Issues and Judgement in an action entitled Sandy Young Hopkins, Laura Hopkins Kirk, Norman Lee Freeman and Blanche Freeman, et als, vs. W. L. Hill, the same being taken from and compared with the original records on file in this office.

Witness my hand and official seal, this 10th day of November, 1944.

Maude Lee Boling
Ass't Clerk Superior Court

REVISED SUPPLEMENTAL DATA

When I wrote "Controversial Mark Hopkins"—and it was accepted by the famous and long-standing Publisher, Greenburg: Publisher—201 East 57th Street, New York City, I was highly elated by the report from "A PUBLISHER'S CONVENTION"—It RAN:

"THERE ARE MANY, MANY BOOKS WHICH NEVER REACH THE SALE VOLUME IN FIGURES THAT YOUR BOOK—'CONTROVERSIAL MARK HOPKINS' ATTAINED AND DERIVED AT. ON THE PUBLICITY SIDE, I WOULD SAY YOUR BOOK RECEIVED MORE AND LARGER REVIEWS THAN 90% OF ALL BOOKS PUBLISHED!"

However in the "REVISED" edition—and after the years of extensive study from 1953-62—I am happy to announce that I have fulfilled a mission, somewhat on the dotted line of a challenge, from some famous history professor who said.

"Mrs. Latta has made a great revelation to the railroad systems and the industrial structure of the United States of America. As time progresses and with her untiring efforts in HER ENDEAVOR TO ESTABLISH THE BIOGRAPHY OF 'TWO GREAT MEN' (MARK HOPKINSES')—there is no doubt in my mind's eye but what she will find—THE WHOLE STORY—AND RESURRECT AND UNRAVEL THE ENTIRE MISSING LINKS IN PERFECTED DOCUMENTED ORDER—

AND, ESTABLISH A TRUE LINEAGE OF PRO-
GENITORSHIP FOR THE 'TWO GREAT AMERI-
CANS,' WHOSE BIOGRAPHIES WERE STOLEN
AND LOST IN SPACE!"

Now, I must admit—: "I NEVER EXPECTED THIS
VISION TO BECOME A REALITY. BUT, IT ACT-
UALLY HAS PERFORMED THAT GOD'S HOLY
MIRACLE—IRRESPECTIVE OF THE BILLIONS
TO COVER UP THE 'STOLEN BIOGRAPHY' AND
'EMPIRE OF WEALTH' THAT MARK HOPKINS—
FROM BEDDING COUNTY, VIRGINIA AND RAN-
DOLPH COUNTY, NORTH CAROLINA, EMASSED
FROM 1852-78!"

Another confession which hurts very deeply and quite
humiliating to confess is the fact: That I really knew little
about the magnitude of the wealth which Mark Hopkins
died, seized, and possessed when I wrote the first edition in
1953. However, by the "DIVINE POWER AND GUID-
ANCE OF GOD"—I AM RICH IN KNOWLEDGE
AND WISDOM NOW ON THE SUBJECT. (MANY
HISTORIES WILL BE WRITTEN ON THE SUB-
JECT IN THE NEAR FUTURE.)

The major confession—which hurts to a superlative de-
gree is the humiliating factor: I GAVE A LOT OF
CREDIT TO THE POSITIONS OF THE SAMUEL
FREDERICK HOPKINS'S LINEAGE—AND THE
"SONS" which WERE ALL IN ERROR. THEY WERE
VAGABONDS AND RESIDING IN SAINT CLAIR,
MICHIGAN—ON THE DATE OF THE DEATH OF

"MY UNCLE'S DECEASE"—MARCH 29th, 1878. NEVER PUT A FOOT ON CALIFORNIA SOIL UNTIL THE FRAUDULENT AND IMPOSTERSHIP SCHEMES HAD BEEN WORKED OUT BY THE SURVIVING PARTNERS, FEDERAL LAND AGENTS, ATTORNEYS, JUDGES, THE ENTIRE REIGN OF JURISPRUDENCE, BANKING SYSTEMS, MONEY EXCHANGERS, WHICH AFFECTED AND EFFECTED THE ENTIRE ECONOMICAL STRUCTURE OF AMERICA AND ABROAD.

NOTE: TO THE READERS

Please see the additions which have been added, discovered, and made available in this "REVISED COPY!"

The pictures of Mark Hopkins are ones made in his younger years. And, had not been made available for my first "Book!"

The errors made in the first book were all due to the fact: That original records were destroyed and supplanted by faked ones in order to establish the "HEIRSHIP" of the New York Lineage.

George T. Davis, Esquire

AUTHOR'S CHARACTER SKETCH ON THE LIFE OF:—GEORGE T. DAVIS, ESQUIRE.

AND, THE ATTEMPT IN SOME MANNER, TO EXPRESS THE AUTHOR'S GRATITUDE AND APPRECIATION FOR ACCEPTING THE POSITION AS DEFENDANT COUNSEL CONDUCIVE TO THE RECOVERY OF THE MARK HOPKINS STOLEN EMPIRE.

Transference of sentiments from the "HEIRS" of the decedent were founded upon one's mutual respect and gratitude that we were able to obtain "RETAINERSHIP OF ONE OF THE NATION'S GREATEST MEMBER'S OF ANY BAR ASSOCIATION"—WHICH PERMEATES "THE LEGAL PRACTICES OF THE CIVILIZED WORLD." Everywhere one goes he hears of the famous "George T. Davis"—in his Thirty Year Battle Against CAPITAL PUNISHMENT.

By Brad Williams: "Author's Note"—he relates the fabulous acquittals like the PRUITT'S. The Caryl Chessman scandal, solely because of belief in a cause. "In the thirty years he has practiced he has practiced criminal law in Brazil, Korea, France, Italy, Germany and the United States. Mr. Davis has defended one hundred eighty-six persons accused of murder. With two exceptions, he has won acquittals for all his clients for whom he was the counsel of record at the inception of the trial."

In the "Channels of Law" remarks are whispered with the greatest profound respect for the efficacious manner in which Mr. Davis litigates his cases.

Many will ask— "What Science and Philosophy of Law does he use and pursue?" He always wins his "CASES"—

and wields the unswerving power to aid the poor and helpless victim to raise his head—from sitting in the chair of the
court room—. At least, he feels that he will receive a rendi-
tion from the judge as a result of the "principles of justice"
characterized by every case history of recordation in his extensive field as a practitioner in the legal profession.

Mr. Davis is highly educated. He graduated from California Law School in 1931. Prior to his collegiate work in
the United States he did extensive study abroad in famous
institutions like Eton, and Oxford, England. In addition to
all his university credentials, he is definitely classified as a
master of languages. While he would tell one that his fluent
speaking languages were German, and Spanish an observer
can detect that when any foreigner walks in to his office—void
of the English speaking language—except for the purposes of
introduction et cetera—that George Davis will spontaneously
begin to make himself understood by speaking clearly and
distinctly in the language of his foreign client.

Another attribute which few people along life's pathway
rarely are endowed with: "A charming and magnetic personality!"—But, George Davis, as all his manifold acquaintances
throughout his world-wide legal practice, will admit is a
possessor of these treasured gifts. When he meets an acquaintance, irrespective of his station in life—he will always
step forward and greet him—"with a beaming smile and extended hand!" He never allows hectic days and hours of
mental and physical labor to deprive him of his equilibrium.

When he enters the court-room; the old cold faced judge
sitting on his throne—silence pervading the entire structure—
faces which look solemn and sad—it is apparent that every-

one—even the "JUDGE" will admit "Here Comes The Rainbow!"—The appearance is characterized and magnetized by his kind expression, and glowing light shining from the eye—which seems to take in the whole world at a glance.

However, these are the true characteristics of George Davis when he appeals to one's better self: "He can be cold-blooded and hard as nails when the occasion demands it. One readily sees the transformance of his personality in a split second. Everyone who really knows his code of legal ethics will admit that he is very impatient with any client who implores him to take a case unless it had its origin imbued with justification somewhere along the line and pathway in the conformity to what one terms 'the great gem of reason in its correlation in the administration of justice!' "—While the years of long hard fought battles against capital punishment may seem somewhat contradictory from the preceding statement: "*It Is Not!*"—

George Davis is not opposed to "punishment!"—He is opposed to "CAPITAL PUNISHMENT!"

I suggest, that each "HEIR" whom I hold Power of Attorney for—would read "Due Process"—this is the true Biography of Mr. Davis.

Mr. Williams also stated another constituent in the manifold juridicial realm of Mr. Davis's profession as a manifesto of his legal career and the departments of the legislative, judicial and executive domain of the Constitution of the United States of America—that there were other propelling factors; which were motivated by a typical distinction in his matchless and unequaled performance in his career as a general practitioner of the legal profession.

The following is the quote: "There is another drive that also motivates George T. Davis, an attitude not restricted exclusively to him, but to which he is dedicated as religiously as he is to the abolition of capital punishment. It is a constant burning resentment against injustice, against what he thinks is a consistent practice of many prosecutors to use the law for political expediency. It is, to George T. Davis, a constant moral obligation to see that justice is served."

He, Mr. Davis, calls this Due Process.

He had an important long distance call one day as I sat in his office—I strolled along the corridor of his office suite, glancing at the various volumes in his collection: One stood predominantly, very much abused by usage. The title read: "The Power of Prayer!"

I then summarized: "Like the student often getting his Latin in college perfected by the candle light—after the other students were forced to turn in by the lights in the 'dorm' and all tucked in slumber land. One eve a competitor wondered where the mystic student gained his power over the others. He snooped and saw the student kneeling over his Latin book.

"His competitor turned away—highly exhilarated over the discovery. 'Now—I see where he gets his margin on us!'"

The same derivation and summarization entered my mind with reference to the Prayer Book and Mr. Davis. I thought in his hard fought battles for justice, principles, standards and ideals which he had characterized and inculcated in his profession. "It just could be his source of 'Power' by which he obtains his margin on other members of his profession!"

Mark Hopkins, the Southerner who made California great and saw Sacramento grow up.

This book is fondly dedicated to the cherished
memories of my beloved parents
Susan Ann Vaughan Cothran
and
William Anderson Cothran

ACKNOWLEDGMENT

I regret that space does not permit me to list the many individuals who have been helpful in assembling the material for this volume.

Special acknowledgment is due the following:

Miss Mary L. Allison, who has collaborated in writing the book.

Miss Eleanor Price, U. S. Government specialist in history, who has contributed helpful advice from the beginning of the undertaking.

Dr. A. C. Jordan, Professor of English at Duke University, who as a licensed attorney has advised on legal aspects.

CONTENTS

ILLUSTRATIONS

FOREWORD

History and its truths have a forceful and persistent habit of exerting themselves. In the daily process of living, history is slowly created and what seems reasonable and valid one day may prove to be false a generation or a century later. The small event or the broad issue is often determined by the men or the forces most powerful, most influential at the time. Thus, problems of justice and of progress in human affairs are settled at the time they occur in the most expedient manner possible. And so history is constantly being shaped and molded by men and groups of men, even as it is formed by shifting economic conditions, changing social values, political circumstances, sudden world catastrophes. As these external affairs shift, so social groups and individuals move from one line of activity or emphasis to another. Those men who believe that the mistakes they made or the selfish acts they performed will be forgotten or forgiven err in this illusion. Sometimes, of course, injustices are permitted to remain in the record. But, fortunately more often than not, the records of history are re-examined, placed in a new perspective, given a new hearing. Only after such re-evaluation can we with integrity say that the history of a past event has been finally recorded.

Though courts and corporations, newspapers and biographies, individuals, partnerships, and societies may presume that a decision once made is a final act, the questions which were raised and left unanswered at the time of the settlement remain to tantalize the curious and to haunt those most directly concerned. When such questions embrace the broad continent of America, stretching from North Carolina to California and back to New York, and involve the security and prosperity of thousands of property owners and share holders, they take on an added significance. They raise the issue of economic justice and call into doubt the legality of methods used by the lower, as well as the higher, courts in disposing of controversial problems.

One such controversial question that has plagued American courts and historians—to be as clear and as direct about it as possible—is: Was the estate of Mark Hopkins, legendary member of the legendary quartette of the Big Four of California railroads, settled and distributed in an equitable and legal manner? Were his vast holdings fully considered in the final disposition?

To ask: "Who are the legitimate heirs of Mark Hopkins?" is to drop a tiny pebble into long quiet, untroubled waters and thus to create an almost endless series of related questions, concentric circles, if you like, which create new circles, new questions, each generating new force to induce a new ripple.

This book is one such pebble.

Hopkins and Stanford Residences

CONTROVERSIAL MARK HOPKINS

FIRST FACTS

When we ask the questions concerning the Mark Hopkins estate, we are not being innovators. Others have asked them; others have placed their claims for proper answers before the courts of the land. And in turn, we ask: "Were the subsequent litigations in the case of the Hopkins wealth founded on any slim possibility of validity? Do those now appealing for a drastic reinterpretation of the known facts have a right to be heard?" We think they do. And we also think that Americans who have always fought for a free and open hearing on any question will agree with us. They too, will want to investigate the life and career of the *real* Mark Hopkins, the Mark Hopkins who has gradually emerged from the dusty generalities of eight decades.

It is ironic to realize that the Mark Hopkins of Califronia, the storekeeper and merchant, the financier and railroad magnate, the owner of a vast empire of land, and the controlling executive of steamship lines, cargo boats, interurban transit companies, ore mines and lumber yards, construction firms, cable cars and docks, should be so little known in a country where individual achievement and personal history are so honored.

Except for such generalities as those written in the obituary columns at the time of his death in 1878—"As a man he was pure; as a friend, sincere; as a citizen, patriotic; as a merchant, honorable"* history has little on which to build a living, vibrant personality. Yet he was unquestionably one of America's leading merchant princes—a builder and possessor of an estate so vast that its total extent and value have never been fully computed. But in the standard encyclopedias of America's leading men and women we find no mention of his name, no reference to his early life, his manhood, his career, his death. Even *The Dictionary of American Biography,* written and published by one of America's leading learned societies—an exhaustive, detailed, admirable contribution to American history—carries no article on Mark Hopkins. Other works, equally scholarly and respected, show the same error of omission. Where volumes do deal with the great railroad builder, we find that their basic, common source has been the highly-colored, non-professional, slim volume of a local raconteur.

Why this strange silence? Presumably (for so much of Hopkins' biography must be founded on presumption) Mark Hopkins never wished his life and his personality to be an enigma. True, he was quiet and unobtrusive, rarely attending large public events and social functions. Compared with the others in the Big Four, Huntington, Stanford, and Crocker, he was an extraordinarily simple man, interested in fulfilling his talents for business organization and a good bargain. While the others chose to dominate the economic, political, and social life of the growing empire of California,

* Sacramento *Bee,* March 28, 1878.

Mark Hopkins was content, it would seem, to go to his office every day, to work diligently, carefully, shrewdly, and then to return home to his simple quarters at night. The others held high public office, traveled across the length and breadth of the United States, made frequent trips to Europe, played host to the fashionable and wealthy society of San Francisco, and lived a life so public that exhaustive and detailed obituaries were written on their deaths, and biographies, memoirs, and perpetual monuments have been fashioned after their deaths.

Yet Mark Hopkins, an essential unit in the closely-knit, carefully guarded empire of capital wealth, land holdings, and transportation facilities, remains a shadowy figure, moving quickly and silently through the existing records, creating, without intention, a historical riddle. His life was quiet, his death sudden, his fortune quickly distributed.

The date of his birth remains unestablished, even as the names of his parents continue to be in dispute. As one reads the several biographical sketches and obituary notices, one discovers that even at the time of his death, no one could with certainty give the name of the city of his birth. The certainties—what there are of them—amount to so little when balanced against the multiple gaps. Where in one account no wife tended a household, in the court room a widow suddenly appears; where no children grieved over his grave, heirs later arise. As suddenly and as mysteriously, lands purchased and duly deeded evaporate in the disposition of the Hopkins estate, even as do the wealth-producing shares in the Southern Pacific Railroad. Just as effectively, the prevailing laws and legal customs of the State of California are quickly overlooked. Eventually, but not quite so effectively, the legal questions of wills and heirs, estates and holdings, and the charges that were made at the time of fraud, connivance, and willful conspiracy are also silenced.

The overwhelmingly pertinent questions of fact remain without sound, proven, indisputable answers. To read the few available biographical sketches of Hopkins is to become involved in a history of railroad building in California, to comprehend the force and strength of the characters who made that empire possible, and to delve into the intricacies of court proceedings. To do these researches is to open the heavy portals guarding a series of related mysteries.

Who was the true Mark Hopkins? What sort of boyhood had he led? What kind of family did he come from and what happened to his mother, his father, and his brothers and sisters after Mark departed from his boyhood home? What lure of adventure, what chance for anonymity or prospect of wealth caused him to leave the Eastern Seaboard and make the arduous journey to California in the uncertain days of the Gold Rush? What training or past experiences had enabled Mark Hopkins to become a noted merchant and to establish a leading hardware store in his adopted home of Sacramento? What personal insecurity or family secret drove him to silence about his past and present family relationships? Why was it that at the time of his death in March, 1878, when the Central Pacific Railroad and its four capitalist founders had achieved worldwide renown for their power, their prosperity, and their ingenuity, virtually nothing was known about the private life and affairs of one of the company's projectors and founders, Mark Hopkins?

The facts that are known and recognized are few. Historians agree that Mark Hopkins reached California soon after the gold bonanza of 1849 and that he joined with Collis P. Huntington in a partnership established for the purpose of running the hardware store of Huntington & Hopkins in Sacramento in the year 1855. The next event, the one that so permanently changed the life of Mark Hopkins, is also accepted by all students in railroad history. In 1861 Mark Hopkins, together with his partner Huntington and two other Sacramento merchants—Charles Crocker and Leland Stanford, as well as with other Sacramento residents, met in an office of that thriving city to listen to a young engineer —Theodore Judah. He was there to explain his plans and hopes for a transcontinental railroad to the few men of the town who had the business acumen and the capital resources to make his dream a reality. As business men, they were also speculators, for in those eventful days in California wealth was made and lost by gambling on an idea, a plot of land, a hill with gold in it, an invention, a money-making scheme. Whatever their motives were, either as a group or as individuals, these leaders could see in Judah's enthusiastic account a possible basis for wealth. Eight men agreed to finance a survey of the proposed railroad—thus giving their support to a project that would change every aspect of American life.

History records that the Central Pacific Railroad was actually started on January 8, 1863, and that on May 10, 1869, its tracks were joined with those of the Union Pacific Railroad at Promontory Point in Utah, to complete the first transcontinental railway line. History also records that during the time of construction—as well as long after—the Central Pacific Railroad was controlled by four men—Huntington, Stanford, Crocker, and Mark Hopkins. History then recounts how the four were not content to control one railroad but worked without a moment's hesitation or a backward glance to gain control of all the other railroads that had been established in the Western states. Nor were the other existing means of transportation safe from their possessive manipulations. Control of competing transportation and haulage companies soon became theirs.

Much is known of the financial arrangements, the political intrigues and pressures brought to bear, and the monopolistic practices indulged in by the leaders of the Central Pacific Railroad. But the full and complete record of every activity in the company's history during the seventeen years that followed that first meeting in Sacramento will probably never be fully known. Whatever it may have been, it is certain that Mark Hopkins was a part of that vital history, attending to his numerous financial duties with diligence and industry.

Meanwhile, the other three capitalists had become richer and richer. As Hopkins' associates became wealtheir, they began to build themselves magnificent mansions, to travel, to buy art works, and to enjoy the fruits of their labors with a life of ease and luxury.

Not, however, Mark Hopkins. As his friends gained power and influence in political circles, Mark Hopkins seemed to retreat more and more into the background. He never sought nor did he ever secure a place in the political limelight of his adopted state or of the nation. As the families of his partners attained social prominence and importance,

Mark Hopkins continued to live modestly and moderately. At the time of his death, in 1878, the newspapers bemoaned the loss of one of the guiding spirits of the Central Pacific, lamenting the passing of one with such thrifty habits, of such good nature, and of such persistence and perseverance. But little was said of his actual life and the important events in the life of any man—such as his birth date, his family origins, his business possessions, etc. True, he was spoken of as one of the great railroad magnates of the West, and a few of the obituaries listed his survivors as a widow and a brother. Other relatives were vaguely referred to, although these reports varied with each obituary. A Mary Sherwood Hopkins and a Moses Hopkins claimed to be his widow and brother, respectively, and thereby stood to inherit the bulk of his fortune, the exact amount of which was not known at the time of his death and has since never been definitively totaled.

In presenting this volume to the public, we hope that the narrative briefly sketched in the foregoing paragraphs can be enriched and completed, thus opening up for public discussion the life and death of Mark Hopkins and the legality of the methods used to settle his estate. Both issues are inevitably and permanently interwoven. This research into the biography of an important American—this attempt to reveal the discrepancies, the ambiguities, and the missing links in the career of a great man and a great railroad—has been carried on in a spirit of humility and impartiality. There has been no attempt to smear or to cry out hysterically against the courts and the corporations. But as the facts

revealed themselves, as one tiny notice in a primary document was discovered, as errors in the secondary material
were recognized, an emotion approaching that of a crusader
did from time to time prevail. History and its meanings,
truth and its need to dominate became paramount and guided
the heart and the hand of the researcher and author.

Without a doubt, numbers of individuals stand to benefit
materially by any new interpretation of the available facts
about Mark Hopkins. Even more individuals may find the
economic basis of their entire lives drastically altered by
any such new interpretation. For the Mark Hopkins Controversy is more than an historical debate; it is a controversy of individuals, of fortunes, of landed estates, and of
capital holdings. Shares in such powerful corporate organ-
izations as the Southern Pacific Railroad, the Central Pacific
Railroad, the Capital Savings Bank of Sacramento, the London and San Francisco Bank, Wells Fargo, and many others
may be in jeopardy. Owners of cattle ranches, wheat fields,
orchards, city blocks, home lots, docks, transit lines, and
cargo boats may find their titles questionable. State and
national histories may be found in error; court proceedings
and legal decisions may be sharply criticized; individual
behavior may be found irresponsible, illegal, even fraudulent.

Yet Americans have never hestitated to listen to legitimate
claims for justice. There is a sufficient number of cases in
which the first decisions of legislatures and courts have been
re-examined to justify this faith in the principles of equal
justice before the law. The American citizen does not like
to be duped. He does not wish to be a party to fraud and

injustice. He wants the whole truth and nothing but the truth, however disturbing and bitter it may be.

Only recently Americans have been shocked to learn of the many and adverse ways in which bribery and corruption can penetrate the institutions of government. They have been astonished to read that from the lowest local level to the highest national bureaus, there has been widespread collusion between dishonest men and public officials. Most Americans are determined to correct these abuses. In previous decades other public scandals have been exposed and corrected. There was the infamous Credit Mobilier in which thousands were cheated of their life's earnings by purchasing watered stock and worthless shares. Writers and reformers and historians assisted materially in the correction of this blight on American economic life. The scandals of the Grant and Harding administrations have been described many times and the corrupting influence and practices of monopolistic firms in the last century have been exposed by journalists and historians. Once brought to their attention, these and similar frauds were fully exposed and terminated by the American people.

This attempt to establish the true identity of Mark Hopkins and to reveal the methods used in disposing of his estate may prove to be another landmark in the never-ending struggle for justice. Surely the problem is as fascinating as it is complicated. One historian has stated of Mark Hopkins: "Less is known of him than of any of his associates."* It is hoped that the new facts brought to light after long years

* Stuart Daggett, *Chapters on the History of the Southern Pacific*, Ronald Press Company, New York, 1922, p. 14.

of diligent, painful, often frustrating, but always absorbing, research will remedy this lamentable historical situation. It is further hoped that these new facts and these new interpretations of established facts will help to end what has been so aptly called "The Mark Hopkins Controversy."

Sacramento, California, 1869.

2

AN INQUIRY INTO A MYSTERY

Of all the questions which surround this historical mystery, there is one fact which is not questionable—Mark Hopkins was a significant and influential American. No one denies that in the figure of Mark Hopkins we have an individual who during his comparatively short life became one of the most powerful financial figures on the Pacific Coast. His ideas, his ambitions, his loyalties, his decisions contributed to one of the major achievements of industrial America— the building of the transcontinental railroad which made the astonishing speed of industrializing America possible. Yet this figure, so recognized and so applauded, has small space in the history books and the reference volumes. Today it is well nigh impossible to gain any detailed, interpretative, and precise information about him as a person or as a force in this great transportation endeavor.

Take from the library shelves any of the reputable American reference books, such as *The Dictionary of American Biography*, the *Dictionary of American History*, *The Americana Encyclopedia*, the *Encyclopedia Britannica*, *Learned's Dictionary of American History*, Beard's *Rise of American Civilization*, and you will discover that nowhere in these exhaustive works does his name even appear!

In those few volumes where his name and career are recorded, the material is by comparsion with other items astonishingly scanty, full of gaps in time and interpretation, uncertain of basic facts, hesitant and faltering in manner. All of these inadequate references rely almost exclusively, not on original material gathered by the individual authors, but on a thin, non-professional sketch written by B. B. Redding of San Francisco and printed in 1881. A local raconteur, Redding in that year got together the little information known about the great magnate, added the vague personal impressions of several local citizens, and issued *A Sketch of the Life of Mark Hopkins.* The other feeble source is the biographical account in the records of the Sacramento Society of California Pioneers. These are the volumes, these the source books from which subsequent writers have taken their cue and their so-called facts! Professional historians have taken little time and less trouble to investigate on their own initiative the deeds and decisions of the great railroad executive. In addition, the few short biographies that have been published show considerable variations with respect to the facts presented and the interpretations made of his role in the railroad business.

Such omissions and gaps may seem to some to be inevitable. And if there are conflicting opinions and contradictory facts about a figure in the past, surely, some will think, such omissions and contradictions have surrounded many another historical figure and event. One may well ask: "Shouldn't gaps in the information about a man who lived in the turbulent, fast-moving, non-recorded days of mid-century California be expected?" When men were too busy building the future to keep accurate accounts of the present, when an empty desert plot could as if overnight become a thriving commercial center, how can a historian account for every event, every personage?

An acceptance of such a situation in history is reasonable. Gaps are inevitable and contradictory interpretations are to be expected. Indeed, intelligent debate about an event is vital to the search for truth. But in revealing the shocking lack of material on Mark Hopkins we are dealing with a different phenomenon. For, remember, he was one of four industrial giants. He was not a lone, shadowy figure going about his deeds in a clandestine fashion. He was a member of an extensive, powerful corporation; he was on a team that pushed economic organization forward into a preeminent position. The other members of this phenomenal team have volumes in great number devoted to them; and the organization they built is described in minute detail. If enough data exists to supply material for hundreds of books and magazine articles on Collis P. Huntington, Leland Stanford, and Charles Crocker, and on the many other individuals concerned with the Central Pacific Railroad, why is there no similar data on Mark Hopkins?

Obviously, Mark Hopkins has never received his share of biographical treatment because so little information about him exists. But the answer to why this should be so is not so obvious. Huntington, Stanford, and Crocker have been given full historical recognition. Even Theodore Judah, the engineer who originated the vision of a transcontinental railroad and who for many years after his sudden and youthful death was neglected by historians and commen-

tators, has been fully recognized and several well-docu-
mented, exhaustive biographies of the engineer are now on
the book shelves. Yet silence continues to envelope the
figure of Mark Hopkins. Where then is the basic source
material on this member of the quartette? Why should
there be documents and records on Huntington, Stanford,
and Crocker, and none on Mark Hopkins?

This lack of original material turns out to be one of the
crucial questions in the Mark Hopkins Controversy. After
twenty years of research on the subject, it is possible to come
to only one conclusion. The usual sources of information
on this man, the materials commonly used by any historian
in building a biography, were destroyed—some by accident,
others by deliberate, conscious act. Individuals and groups
who have not wished the critical eyes of history to examine
the events of the past have deliberately, willfully, and with
evil intent destroyed the vital sources of historical information. This is a stern and damning judgment, but the only
one possible when time and time again documents cited in
court house archives and state library catalogues cannot be
found or are listed as "missing," "lost," "whereabouts unknown." It is certainly more than an accident to discover that
an original record, housed behind the heavy doors of the
National Archives, has been indisputably altered. Or, again,
to find that a vitally important paper is torn just at the place
where an authenic signature should appear is more than
disconcerting; it points the finger of accusation at those who
have concerted together to destroy information of a character
that might have resolved the mystery of Mark Hopkins.
In so far as it was possible, the significant data on Mark Hop-

kins and the disposition of his estate has been systematically and relentlessly destroyed. Other equally important material has been distorted in such a manner as to confuse and confound anyone who might be tempted to evaluate the life and property of Mark Hopkins.

Having stated this shocking fact, the next question is inevitable. Why should anyone have troubled to destroy the documents around a man's life? Why should national and state archives agree to a confiscation of the very records entrusted to them and thus contribute their share to historical errors and confusions? And, again, how could such destruction and confiscation be accomplished? And, finally, the last question to be asked revolves around the existence of much material on the other three. If documents on Mark Hopkins were destroyed, why not those on Huntington, Stanford, and Crocker? If the motive in such destruction were to rescue the reputation and legality of the Central Pacific Railroad, why weren't the tell-tale data on the other three removed? Surely, they were as deeply enmeshed in the dubious manipulations of the transportation firm as was Mark Hopkins. Why then should only the Mark Hopkins documents and records have disappeared?

If one analyzes the peculiar circumstances surrounding the Central Pacific Railroad and its partners in the eventful year of 1878, one finds the answer to these related questions. The year in which Hopkins died—1878—was a critical one for the railroad. Developing and expanding and affluent as it was, its financial condition was deplorable. The government bonds which had so largely financed the expensive construction of the line during the 1860's were now in ar-

rears; yet there was no ready cash in the treasury to repay
these loans, or even to pay the mounting interest on the
bonds.   Debts to builders, suppliers, banks, and mortgage
holders were rapidly accumulating, but the partners made
no effort to meet these debts.   Profits were still being taken
out of the firm, but debts were not being paid.   In addition,
the railroad was beginning to come in for its share of public
criticism for its decidedly monopolistic practices.   Political
representatives were listening to the grievances of those who
had been pushed aside in the vigorous fight for economic
power and control waged by the transportation corporation.
One committee had already been appointed by an aroused
Congress to look into the methods and financial procedures
that were to make the Central Pacific Railroad a giant corporation.

In that critical year of 1878 it was absolutely essential that
the stocks and bonds of the railroad be maintained at their
high value on the stock market and that the reputation of the
organization be such as to continue to win public support and
tacit political approval.   It was imperative for continued
development that the company present a solid financial front.
Equally vital was the friendship of members of the national
and state legislatures.   Thus some way had to be found to
silence the critics and hold back the creditors—a way that
would not limit the profits of the Big Four nor change their
successful methods of domination.

On the very day that Mark Hopkins died so suddenly
and so far away from his usual residence, the Congress of
the United States was investigating the finances of the Central Pacific Railroad and debating with considerable heat the

passage of an act that would permit the railroad to establish
a sinking fund to pay its debts.   Reports of this legislative
debate occupied prominent spots in metropolitan newspapers
and occasioned numerous editorial comments throughout the
press of the nation.   Even at that early date in our career
as a growing nation, Americans knew about and were concerned with the financial structure and management practices
of one of the country's most important enterprises.   Because
of this public interest, the Big Four were exerting every
effort possible to maintain their envied position of power
and wealth.   The Big Four had to quiet the grumblings of
the public, soften political censure, and meet their financial
obligations without jeopardizing for a moment their individual earnings.

Into this critical moment came the news of the death of
Mark Hopkins.   There was little time to grieve for the loss
of a business associate.   Of more importance than the death
of an individual was the disposition of his holdings in the
tenuously financed corporation.   The manner in which his
capital wealth and land holdings, as well as his numerous
shares in the railroad, would be distributed, was decisive.   If
his estate were to be divided among his heirs, then the
financial status of the railroad would be weakened percep-
tibly and there would be little to hold off the mounting tide
of public opinion and government investigation.   If, however, the holdings of Mark Hopkins were to remain under
the control of the remaining members of the quartet, then
the great Hopkins wealth and his share of the profits could
be used to bolster the faltering financial structure and thus

return the corporation to public favor, government approval, and strong economic status.

Obviously one answer to their problems was the distribution of Hopkins' share in the railroad companies among the remaining three, where it could remain under their perpetual guidance and control. Was it equally easy to make the answer materialize? Though it may have seemed difficult at the beginning, subsequent events proved that the solution to their multiple problems was comparatively easy. To men accustomed to ruthless deeds to gain their ends, the transferral of the major portion of Hopkins' holdings to the benefit of the Central Pacific Railroad was not as hard as it might have been for more scruplous men. By acquiring the Mark Hopkins estate, Huntington, Crocker, and Stanford could be sure of continuing their control of the railroad as well as of the multiple other financial schemes and operations in which the four had been engaged. To permit the estate to be distributed among heirs not associated with the company was unthinkable; every device, legal and illegal, had to be used to prevent such a calamity.

It may seem harsh to attribute such motives to three respectable members of California society, but the situation was grave and critical. Such behavior would not be new in a country where other men's wealth had been misappropriated after their death, nor was it new to Huntington, Stanford, and Crocker who had grown used to wielding their power and position to gain control of other men's just shares in their common undertaking. Their treatment of two of their associates, Theodore Judah and David Colton, is an example of their practiced ruthlessness.

Here then we have the motive for the debated settlement
of the Hopkins fortune and for the subsequent and systematic
destruction of most of the information about Mark Hopkins
and his affairs.   A motive for committing fraud did exist.
The three railroad capitalists wanted to protect their vast
and profitable holdings—at whatever cost to their integrity,
to their sense of justice, to their reputation.   Once having
determined to gain control of the estate, the rest of the deeds
followed easily.   And so we return to the question of the
altered, the destroyed, the missing biographical documents.

An individual or a group of individuals who had been
party to a fraudulent act would necessarily have to cover
their tracks.   One sure way of doing that was to destroy
all evidence that might shake their position.   Only they
knew how significant were the biographical documents per-
taining to Mark Hopkins, for around the life of this man
centered the question of the settlement of his estate and all
the subsequent deeds and commitments.   In order to ensure
maximum protection to their fraud, thorough destruction of
the pertinent biographical material had to be accomplished.
For it was and is the confusion surrounding the life of Mark
Hopkins which has continued to make a new settlement of
the issues of the estate impossible or, at the most, exceedingly
difficult and complicated.   Only by agreeing that some one
or some group deliberately destroyed all documents that
might have contributed to a true biography can we account
for the fact that there is no historical material on Mark
Hopkins.

It is common knowledge among California old-timers,
who were interviewed and who were familiar with the gossip

and the conjectures and the memories of others, that millions of dollars were probably spent to falsify the records and thus make it impossible for any one ever to know with a certainty substantiated by unimpeachable documents that could stand up in a court of law the true nature of Mark Hopkins' estate, the dubious justice used to distribute it, and, most important of all, the true biography of one of America's leading industrialists. In fact, it was an attorney, hired to contest the court action of the North Carolina heirs of Mark Hopkins, who in 1944, in the presence of witnesses, remarked to his legal opponents: "I know—and so does the legal profession of California—that the settlement of the Mark Hopkins estate was the biggest fraud ever perpetrated on any group of heirs or the State of California; but we hope that time has cured it."

Time, however, has not cured it. And in the end it will be time that moves to the side of justice.

There are a few other points which must be stressed before moving on to the central problem of this volume. One is the comparative ease with which the Hopkins documents were destroyed. But we need only to remember the power and influence and wealth of the Central Pacific Railroad and its chief executives. This was no small private corporation fighting for its existence in a competitive or hostile environment. Every one in America wanted railroads and thus anyone who could provide such transportation was automatically raised to a position of prestige and power. This power was especially great in the State of California. It is readily accepted by all historians and political commentators that many of the actions and decisions of the state legislature, the national government, and the courts were dictated by the powerful railroad tycoons. It was not until Hiram W. Johnson was elected Governor of California in 1911 that the domineering hold of the railroads on state and national affairs began to be broken. For such personages the petty bribing of law clerks, minor individuals employed in the state and national archives, and other such tools was a trifling matter.

One other question remains to be settled before the central theme can be introduced, and that is the comparative abundance of material on the other three railroad executives. True, some significant material is missing so that even today it is impossible to tell the full story of the Central Pacific Railroad. Financial records have been lost; other significant transactions were never permanently recorded; full statements of the wealth of the three have never been made. Still, the basic facts on Huntington, Stanford, and Crocker are available and easily accessible to all. The only conclusion that can be drawn is that there was no need to hide the facts— at least not the same kind of need that resulted in the mystery of Mark Hopkins' life. Though the remaining Big Three might desire to have certain facts of their past manipulations forgotten and obliterated by time, they wanted their *personal* lives fully portrayed and glorified. Indeed, all three individuals delighted in granting interviews to press reporters, sanctioned official biographies, offered to libraries favorable records and documents. Ample letters and journals have been left by them, documents which reveal much about their personalities, their early efforts, their successful financial ventures. The newspapers of their time are full

of accounts of their activities in the business, social, and
political world.

And then we come to a strange gap in the information.
Nowhere in the material on or by the three surviving railroad associates are there accounts of their missing member.
Even mention of his name is remarkably rare when one
stops to imagine how much they really must have known
about him to have associated with him so intimately and
for so long. They were equally reticent in describing the
role of Mark Hopkins played in forming and shaping and
guiding the giant corporation. Of course, they acknowledged that such a partner existed and took part in the early
struggles and formative period. However, when they came
to speak or to write of Mark Hopkins in any kind of detail,
generalities took to place of specific remarks. They general-
ize about his character, his personal idiosyncrasies, his first
years in Sacramento. But they do not record their thoughts
on Mark Hopkins' death; they give no official statement of
his financial status in the company; they have no word to
say on his heirs. Not one of his associates gave a statement
to the press, to biographers, to the courts concerning the
shares of railroad stock held by Mark Hopkins at the time
of his death. They unhesitatingly gave full accounts of how
Mark Hopkins had joined them in their first organization for
a transcontinental railroad; but after that, a silence falls on
them all. They were free with their accounts of the period
in the 1870's when the brave new venture was in its formative stage; and they were also vocal in their descriptions of
their individual responsibilities and programs in the decades
after 1870, but in this latter period there is no record of the

Moses Hopkins, brother of Mark Hopkins.

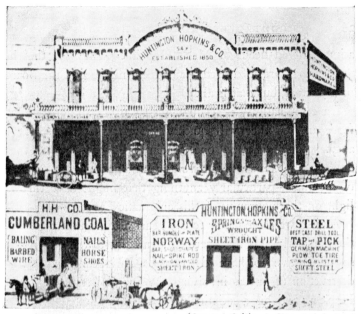

The Sacramento store of Huntington, Hopkins & Co., formerly 54 K Street, now 220-228 K Street. The store extended through to the next block; the lower part of the picture shows the L Street frontage.

Capitol at Sacramento during the inauguration of Governor John B. Weller, January 8, 1858

acknowledged deeds of Mark Hopkins. They say that he was the treasurer of the company and a member of the Board of Directors, but that is all.

An examination of the manuscripts of Huntington, Stanford, and Crocker will quickly show this strange discrepancy. There is only one conclusion to be drawn: they deliberately connived to avoid all mention, all discussion of the man—particularly anything that might have thrown light on the biography of this enigmatic figure.

And so we come closer to the heart of the matter. It was the personal items that were so significant to these men and so imperative to have destroyed. It is conceivable that destruction of papers involving the financial status of Mark Hopkins and his association with the complicated workings of the great corporation would be destroyed in order to protect the reputation of the company at a critical time in its history. If destruction of such information was necessary in order to gain control of his holdings, why should such destruction extend to the personal details of his life? Why did the Big Three make of Mark Hopkins an enigma, unknown to his neighbors and to future historians? The successful obliteration of Hopkins' biography was the inevitable necessity of their prime need—to gain control of his estate. If they were to do this, it was imperative that his life be equally under their control.

With this conclusion the Mark Hopkins Controversy becomes two-fold: one, the dubious manner of estate disposition; two, the systematic removal of all documents of a biographical nature. To perceive the way in which these two issues are unalterably connected is to find the answers to all the questions which have been asked in this volume as well as in the courts of law and in the minds of historians. Such a connection is the only one that can give answers to: How could directors of a company, no matter how powerful, gain access to the private papers of a man? How could a company take over the disposition of a vast estate, since none of the officials most intimately involved were relatives of the deceased man? How was it possible for the courts to distribute a man's estate to his business associates unless a will so specified? And how could such a will, presuming for the sake of fair argument that such existed, deny all mention of heirs? Why shouldn't such a will be contested? How was it possible for individuals previously unrecognized to be granted unspecified inheritances by the courts? And, finally, how did the personal papers of Mark Hopkins disappear so suddenly, so completely?

The first series of questions involves the settlement of an estate. Was the settlement legal and just? Were the prevailing legal codes adhered to? Did the legitimate heirs receive their proper inheritances? Did the men dominating the affairs of the Central Pacific Railroad and the Southern Pacific Railroad have an extra-legal share in determining the settlement of the estate? Was a fraud committed, and if so, how?

The second series of questions revolves around the central character in the drama—Mark Hopkins, himself. Who and what was he? Why is his life and death a mystery? For what reasons and to what purposes have the biographical facts been obscured and neglected? Was there fraud, too, in the account of his life?

A solution to the first series of questions will hold the clue to the solution of the second.

Many will in the future, as they have in the past, declare correctly that in the settlement of the Mark Hopkins estate the names of Huntington, Stanford, and Crocker do not appear. None was ever appointed executor of the estate, nor did any of them receive directly from the courts outright grants of funds, lands, or stocks. Such a fact, of course, mitigates against the charge of fraud. But against such a strong fact, there is an equally strong opposing set of circumstances. The substantial portion of Mark Hopkins' estate did eventually and indirectly fall into the hands of the remaining three members of the railroad quartet. Here are but a few of the ways in which the fortune was gradually acquired: There are, for instance, records of huge uncollected debts which were not included in the original inventory of the estate. These debts, advanced by all four, belonged to all four, and when one died, it does not follow that the payments go only to the three, but by law they should go to the estate of the fourth, as well. For a second instance, there is much known property belonging to Mark Hopkins that was not included in the final description and disposition of his estate. To this very day, this property has never been cleared through the courts. In addition, there are land deeds that were made over to Collis P. Huntington before the estate was even officially settled. These deeds were turned over to Huntington by a purported heir of Mark Hopkins, whose right to do such an act has never been tested.

In addition to these documents, there are many instances of circumstantial evidence indicating more than a reasonable doubt that a fraud in the evaluation and distribution of the estate was committed and that the three remaining members of the executive board of the Central Pacific Railroad were intimately and deeply involved in the enactment of this fraud.

Such involvement leads then to a wider circle of participants in the duplicity and injustice. For Huntington, Stanford, and Crocker to have benefited from the settlement, others, closer perhaps to the deceased, must have been willing. Even with the help of such versatile associates as David Colton, E. H. Miller, Jr., and B. B. Redding, the three railroad magnates could not have won such a favorable court settlement without the aid of those claiming blood relation to Mark Hopkins. Keeping in mind that there is a controversy over the historical person of Mark Hopkins as well as over the disposition of his estate, it is logical to conclude that it took more than money and power to achieve mystery, confusion, and profits. It required a close personal relationship and a long-standing personal knowledge of the central figure. In brief, only a relative could furnish both the legitimate claim to the estate and the necessary information about his personal life.

It is the contention of this volume that a relative of Mark Hopkins was involved in the fraud. The claim is offered that a relative assisted in the unjust settlement and contributed to the confusion surrounding the lifetime of Mark Hopkins.

On the surface, this would seem to be a fantastic proposition. But an examination of the evidence beneath the surface shows how cogent, how pivotal this proposition really is. It is known that Mark Hopkins had a younger brother, one Moses Hopkins. It is this relative who so actively concerned himself in the dubious and still debated settlement of the estate, and it is he who assisted in drawing the false and inadequate portrait of his brother.

To explain how a blood relative, a brother, could have committed such an infamy, it is necessary once more to go beneath the surface and to find there a man of unstable character and a long history of behavior and reactions outside the normal social pattern. His life had been strange, indeed, and his character and personality were equally extraordinary. By combining this type of personality with the material benefits he might gain by joining in a conspiracy, we have the answer to how a brother could have consented to the scheme.

All agree that the Moses Hopkins mentioned in obituaries, estate settlements, and subsequent history books was the brother of Mark Hopkins, the railroad entrepreneur. It is also known that at the time of Mark Hopkins' death, this same individual was receiving a monthly allowance of $250 from his brother Mark—an exceedingly generous gift in those days. There would seem to be enough evidence to show that this sum was to be paid regularly to Moses out of Mark's income for the remainder of Moses' life.

Yet, generous as this provision was, it could not compare with the vast sums available in Mark Hopkins' estate. It would have taken a strong-willed, highly virtuous, and affectionate brother to have resisted the temptation to connive with others in order to get substantially more resources. We know that Moses Hopkins was not such a man. His will had been weakened long before the death of his brother. He was mentally and spiritually a broken man, ready to accept any offer that would insure his economic security. Since all the circumstances surrounding the death of Mark Hopkins were favorable to fraud, Moses could see no risk to his joining in the conspiracy.

And what of the other heirs, the other members of Mark Hopkins' family? Did they, too, join in the fraudulent scheme? Everything points to their innocence. There is no evidence to show that they even knew of his death. They never learned of the circumstances surrounding his death, nor those involved in the settlement of his estate. They did not even know of the vast wealth possessed by their brother Mark, nor of the special and far-reaching power of the railroad with which he was connected. The world, the newspapers of the times, the journals, the histories refer to only one brother. For all intents and purposes, Moses was the only brother of Mark and the only close family member intimately associated with Mark during the significant last thirty years of his life. It was natural that a misinformed world should accept without hesitation all that Moses might choose to say about his brother and his brother's estate. It was to him that all turned for authoritative information concerning his famous brother.

With these facts before us we can now make the second proposition. Moses Hopkins was the key figure in the double conspiracy—to deprive the legitimate heirs of their share of the Mark Hopkins estate and to confound and confuse future investigators in their search for an accurate biography of Mark Hopkins.

It was a daring and audacious plan, but the profits were enormous enough to risk the dangers of possible future detection. The principals were sure of their financial, political, and legal power to prevent and persistent of systematic questioning and investigation. In the figure and person of Moses Hopkins they had a perfect protective covering for their nefarious plans. Discontented, willing to be silent in exchange for wealth, Moses gave to the group a perfect "front," an alibi, if you like, with which to confront all those who might ask for more thorough search before settlement of the estate.

There was yet another circumstance favorable to their deeds. There existed in Sacramento at the time of Mark Hopkins' death another Hopkins family. Though not related in any way to the subject of this book, the family was a prominent one and one with several members in various important positions with the Central Pacific Railroad. One of them even worked in the treasury department of the corporation, had occasion to sign checks and company documents, and to testify to minor transactions. Here, then, was another circumstance favorable to the fraudulent undertaking.

Thus another one of our propsitions is that this family, this second Hopkins clan, willingly and with complete knowledge of the facts entered into the scheme. It was their presence and their cooperation which contributed so much to the success of the fraud. By claiming the railroad magnate as their true brother and uncle and thus qualifying as legitimate heirs they could share in the great fortune and in payment cooperate in the distortion of biographical facts.

It was stated earlier in this chapter that Moses Hopkins was the only close living relative of Mark Hopkins at the time of his death, and newspaper statements of the time corroborate this fact. Yet in subsequent days Moses Hopkins acknowledged the existence of this second Hopkins family and claimed it as his own! Though one account gave to Mark only one brother, later accounts revealed that Moses claimed brotherhood with a Samuel Frederick and an Ezra Augustus, both members of a Hopkins family. This undisputed and major discrepancy is the most significant fact in this plea for a re-examination of the Mark Hopkins Controversy.

What, then, were the motives back of Moses' scandalous inconsistencies? The first is obvious—wealth! To achieve immediate material comfort he was willing to fabricate, to distort, to destroy. He wanted to conceal the true history of his brother Mark, to cover up for all time his own family background and his own career, thus achieving his greedy goal. Because both he and Mark had consistently refused to discuss their origins or their early life, it was a simple matter, comparatively, for Moses to claim his relationship with the second Hopkins family of Sacramento.

It is pertinent to inquire into why Moses and Mark Hopkins were reluctant to reveal the story of their early years. There is now before us certain evidence (which will be given in its entirety later in this work) to prove that Moses Hopkins was a convicted criminal and an escaped one. He had successfully evaded the law in his home state of North Carolina and after that never again discussed his early life before coming to Sacramento. His brother Mark joined him in this

necessary reticence. Thus we have another motive for Moses'
deceit. He had to preserve himself from police action on
the part of his native state. He never, even if the fortunes
of those close to him were at stake, could reveal his connection with his true relatives; since such a revelation would
bring the law down on him. By placing himself and thereby
his brother Mark in a different Hopkins family, Moses effectively altered history and gave Mark Hopkins a new and
different family background, a new and different place of
birth. Divorcing himself from all sense of family loyalty
and family responsibilty, Moses denied the existence of his
true family and assumed kinship with a completely different,
absolutely unrelated Hopkins family—a family originating
in New York! Of course, Moses thus had to share some
of the fortune with others, but it was more profitable for him
thus to share with a few easily controlled "heirs" than to
survive on the known monthly stipend Mark had provided
for him or to share with the seven legitimate heirs in his true
family in North Carolina.

How then did the courts accept this fraud, this discrepancy in accounts, this confusion in facts? Only because of
yet another favorable circumstance—the existence not only
of a second Hopkins family, but also of another individual
named Mark Hopkins who was employed in the treasury
department of the Central Pacific Railroad! This most fortunate, timely, simple circumstance gave the scheme the
necessary push toward success. With such a fact the gigantic fraud could be perpetrated—an estate could be wrongly
distributed, a man's biography could be wrongly preserved.
With a single blow the two historical injustices could be

Sacramento water front, 1867.

Completion Date of First Transcontinental Railroad in U. S.

molded, particularly since the second Mark Hopkins, the member of the New York family and the associate in the Central Pacific Railroad, had died shortly before the railroad magnate.

The final clue to the controversy has been revealed. Moses Hopkins, brother of the central figure in this volume, for all the good and sufficient personal reasons, plotted with the kin of the New York Hopkins to claim the entire Mark Hopkins estate, to share it to a limited degree with these illegitimate heirs, and with the aid and skill of the powerful heads of the Central Pacific Railroad to win a favorable settlement in the courts of California. Since both history and the courts had to be deceived, a single man was created out of the lives, the fortunes, the careers of two separate, unrelated individuals! As far as history is concerned, the two men became one. As far as the courts were concerned, the fortunes of the one went to the heirs of the other, excepting, of course, the amount that was given to Moses Hopkins, true brother of Mark.

This conclusion has been reached not without trepidation, not without humility before the facts, not without due regard for the mounting circumstantial evidence, and never without persistent, unfaltering, and exhaustive research and study. But it is this proposition, this double-image, which we intend to present.

3

A GENTLEMAN FROM THE SOUTH

When the fateful telegram from S. S. Montague, chief engineer for the Central Pacific Railroad, reached the office of Leland Stanford and was then transmitted to the Sacramento press, the citizenry were shocked at the passing of one of their most prominent members. On March 30, 1878, they learned of the death of Mark Hopkins while resting at Yuma, Arizona Territory. But they learned little else about the great pioneer and builder. His death was recorded, his loss to the community and to the West was promptly recognized, but his life was still kept a mystery. There were lengthy obituaries, but none carried the usual details of birth, family, and other biographical details. Full as they were of praise for Mark Hopkins' character and moral stature, none could tell the reader how the magnate had passed his days, or how he had accumulated his fortune, or how great that fortune was.

One reporter who obviously admired Hopkins and wished to do honor to his memory by writing an appreciative article commented unhappily: "But though books and pamphlets and railway guides may be searched through in vain in order to obtain a true idea of the man and his works, yet the people knew the modest man for what he was. They knew and they know today, when he lies cold and speechless in his bier, that though printers' ink and historians' pens have not glorified his name, it is still an ineffaceable factor in the history of the State. It is written on every line of that stupendous work which winds and curves from San Francisco to Omaha; it is written in the Tehachapi Pass and on the Summit of the Sierras, but more than all it is written in the hearts of the people of Sacramento, the city he loved and where he was beloved. *It is difficult to say much of his personal life* (author's italics) further than what he has, from time to time, told in a modest, quiet, dignified manner to his personal friends. And from these few and irregular tales, together with what the people know of his life here, these points are collated."* The reporter then goes on to repeat what the "records of the Sacramento Society of California Pioneers show."

(Courtesy California Historical Society)

There were less than one hundred inhabitants in
Sacramento in 1850.

The records of this society, however, refer to the Mark Hopkins of New York and do not cover the life of the Mark Hopkins of North Carolina, the co-founder and director of

* Sacramento *Bee*, March 29, 1878.

the Central Pacific Railroad. Thus the reporter for the Sacramento *Bee* succeeded in revering the spirit of the railroad magnate, but failed completely to disclose the facts of his life. The true and significant details concerning Mark Hopkins, his family and his background, have never been fully disentangled and presented to the public. It is the hope of the author that at last the two individuals, each named Mark Hopkins and each connected for a number of years with the Central Pacific Railroad, will be distinguished from each other, and their complete and accurate biographies detailed inso far as the existing documents and records make it possible. Neither man has received a just treatment from history and the courts. This volume hopes to correct this injustice.

The California capitalist, who was among the first to envision and actively support the construction of the transcontinental railroad, was born in Richmond County, Virginia. He moved with his family when still a young boy to North Carolina. Here he spent his childhood and early youth. Of English and Scottish stock, Marks' parents were pioneer farmers, and like so many of the Southern white farmers and freeholders of that period in American history, they were in the habit of moving frequently, ever seeking virgin soil as they edged westward toward the Great Smoky Mountains. Soon after their son Mark was born, the Hopkins family departed from Virginia and moved into Person County, North Carolina. A few years later they were again on the move, this time south into the adjoining Orange County. Some time later they moved southwest into Randolph County. Here in New Hope Township, along the Crow Creek, the Hopkins family settled permanently. Even today there are many descendants of the original Hopkins settlers who own property and live in this area of North Carolina. Among the deeds in the Office of the Register of Deeds in Randolph County is one made by Edward Hopkins to several of his sons, giving them parts of the original Hopkins homestead.

This Hopkins pioneer family of the South had its roots in Scotland. Daniel Martin Hopkins, grandfather of Mark, the railroad builder, was born in Edinburgh. He and his brother, Marcus Hopkins, immigrated to the American colonies, as did so many other Scotch Presbyterians during the troubled reigns of the Georges. Marcus settled in the bluegrass region of Kentucky, near the present city of Frankfort. Daniel Martin was attracted to the more rugged region of the North and settled in New England. At the beginning of the Revolutionary War this same Daniel Martin met and married Sarah Longfellow, a cousin of Colonel Longfellow, father of the New England poet, Henry Wadsworth Longfellow. The young couple lived out their lives in eastern Vermont, rearing a family of four sons—Edward, James, Samuel, and Dennis. Of these children, Edward— or Ned or Neddie, as he was always known to the members of his family—was the most adventurous. He it was who caught the western fever and like so many other New England young men of his time wanted to see the other parts of the expanding American continent, to take up new lands in the virgin, uninhabited regions of the new nation. Thus, while still in his teens, Ned Hopkins left his comfortable family home to seek his fortune. He knew of his uncle Marcus and it was for his home in Kentucky that Ed set out.

Such a trip was difficult and hazardous, but the possible dangers were far outweighed by the chance for change and independence. Thus it was that in due time Ed presented himself to his Uncle Marcus and began a new life on the Kentucky plantation.

Uncle Marcus was pleased to have the young, energetic Ned. The livestock farm could always use the services of an enthusiastic, hard-working young man. For his part, young Ned Hopkins found the rolling acres and the fine grazing land to his liking and gladly consented to settle down on the Kentucky plantation and to share his life and work with his uncle. He found that he preferred the graceful two-story colonial home to the severe New England home of his parents. He enjoyed working in the temperate climate of the South and liked the warm friendly spirit of the free farmers of Kentucky. But perhaps of all the attractions in Kentucky none was of more importance than the presence of a lovely Southern girl named Hannah Crow. Shortly after Ned arrived, he met this winsome girl; soon the two young people were in love and wanted to marry. But this was contrary to the wishes of their families.

While Ned was of sturdy pioneer family, of limited means and simple culture, Hannah was of the Southern aristocratic family of extensive means. She had been raised in the elaborate, cultured home of her grandfather, Moses Chambers, a North Carolina field officer of Revolutionary War fame. Her Father, James Monroe Crow, had been killed in one of the battles with the British, and her grandfather had taken care of Hannah from her infancy. An aristocratic slaveholder, he was not at all pleased that his favorite granddaughter, the child he had reared in comfort and security, should become associated in marriage with the son of a simple farmer. To him, Ned Hopkins was a nobody as well as a poor body. There was no question in his mind of permitting the two young people to marry.

Nor did the Hopkins family favor the match. In their opinion Ned was too young (he was only twenty at the time) and had too few resources with which to marry and support a young wife, particularly a girl accustomed since birth to the best standards of living. Though both families had cogent arguments in their favor and continued to raise objections to the match, the two young people insisted on seeing each other, forced their points of view on the bitter and stubborn family heads, and eventually were married. Neither family blessed the union. As they left the village church after their wedding, prospects for the young couple were black. Neither family had given the usual financial assistance to Ned and Hannah, nor did they give their moral support. In fact, Colonel Chambers was so angered and disappointed in his granddaughter's choice of a spouse that for many, many years he refused to see his grandchild or to have anything to do with her husband.

Fortunately, Uncle Marcus soon regretted his initial antagonism to the married couple. Learning that their first months together had been difficult and insecure, with little funds and small hope for additional income, he invited the young people to come share his home with him. He was a bachelor and quite alone in the world and, as he wrote Ned and Hannah, he would welcome their love and companionship. Happily, Ned returned to the plantation with his bride and began once again to work at the skill of farming and earning a living for his wife and family. Soon the other members of Ned's family forgave the young man for his rash and independent act and welcomed the young Hannah into the Hopkins family; but Colonel Chambers never fully reconciled himself to the marriage and only as the marriage proved successful did he accept his granddaughter back into the family circle.

After the first stormy and insecure months of the courtship and marriage, Hannah Crow and Edward Hopkins settled down to a productive and happy life. They were soon able to Leave Uncle Marcus, establish their own farm, and raise happy, healthy children. Their first children were born in Virginia and their later ones in North Carolina. In all, twelve children were born to Ned and Hannah: Joseph, James, John, Martin, Mark, Moses, Joshua, Prudence, Elizabeth, Annie, Rebecca, and Annias. Of these seven sons and five daughters, two, Joshua and Annias, died in infancy. Another daughter, Elizabeth, who never married, died in her twenties before any of the others. The nine remaining children all grew to full adulthood and lived long lives. With the exception of Mark and Moses, the Hopkins children remained in or near North Carolina for the duration of their lives, marrying and rearing large families. The two exceptions to this family pattern were Mark and Moses, who in 1845 left their home state for California where they lived until their respective deaths. Neither of them had any children.

Mark Hopkins was born on September 3, 1814, twin of Annie Hopkins. Three years later, in 1817, a sixth son was born to Hannah and Edward Hopkins, and in honor of her grandfather and uncles, both of whom were named Moses Chambers, the mother called this son, her youngest, Moses Treadway Hopkins. Later investigation showed that during his lifetime, Moses Hopkins was the only white American citizen at the time with this unusual name. This peculiar fact in the Census Records was to be a fateful piece of evidence in the later reexamination of historical fact.

Although the birth of Mark Hopkins and that of his brothers and sisters cannot be found recorded in any registry office in North Carolina or Virginia, there was the usual family Bible in which all these dates and names were carefully and lovingly noted. That there should be no official record of these births is not at all surprising, since in the nineteenth century, particularly in the frontier regions of the South, there was as yet no uniform nor legally-required procedure for recording births and deaths. The family Bible was the accepted volume for recording the events in a family's history, especially the birth dates and death dates of each member. Nevertheless, there are deeds in the Register's Office of Randolph certifying to the fact that Hannah and Edward Hopkins owned a sizable homestead on Crow Creek in that county and that parts of that property were eventually deeded to several of their sons.

Many witnesses in Randolph County have sworn in the Superior Court and their evidence has been accepted to the fact that they saw and well remembered the Hopkins family Bible in which the genealogy of the clan was carefully detailed. One witness, Mrs. Sula Koppelmeyer, told the court:

Q. Did you ever see the Edward and Hannah Hopkins Bible?

A. Yes, it was in the possession of Aunt Betsy when she lived at our home.

Q. Do you know where that Bible is?

A. Yes, it burned up in my Uncle Nelson Russell's house.

Q. Did you see the names in that old Bible of the children of Edward Hopkins and Hannah Crow Hopkins?

A. Yes, sir. Many, many times. Told my fortune in the Bible; shut it up and see when it would come to pass.

Q. Did you see Mark Hopkins' name in there?

A. Yes, sir.

Q. Did you see Annie Hopkins' name in there?

A. I did, and Mark and Moses and Aunt Annie and my grandmother, Prudence, and Rebecca and Elizabeth.

Q. State whether or not you noticed anything in there relative to the similarity of dates as to the birth of Mark and Annie.

A. Yes, sir. I noticed they were both the same date, and I didn't understand that, and I asked Aunt Betsy, "Why are these two children the same date, Mark Hopkins and Annie Hopkins?" and she says, "Why, honey, those were twins." I says, "Why didn't they name them twin names?" She says, "I can't tell you that."

Q. Do you remember the date of their birth?

A. Yes, sir, 1814; I am positive.

It was inevitable that Mark Hopkins' early years should center around his home with its struggles, its successes, its joys, and its sorrows. As a youngster he moved with his parents from the comparatively civilized area of eastern Virginia to the western frontier of North Carolina. For awhile he was in Person and Orange counties, and then finally he settled in Randolph County. The Hopkins farm extended along the eastern bank of Crow Creek, now known as Big Creek, and included more than 220 acres of meadows, woodlands, orchards, and crop lands. Several small streams meandered through the rolling acres and together with a number of springs helped to keep the area green and productive throughout the year. The orchard was a particular source of pride to the owners, and several old-timers remembered in recent years the tasty apples that could always be found on the Hopkins' trees.

Mark's youth was not unlike that of any other farm boy of his time and place. A boy was expected to work to help his family in all the many daily chores of the farm. By the time a boy was in his teens he was doing a man's full day's work. In later years Mark Hopkins' associates and acquaintances frequently remarked on his devotion to the task then before him, his persistence and energy in handling the many details as well as the important decisions. They remembered the industry and care he devoted to the smallest task. One can be sure that this apitude and love of hard work had been inculcated in Mark at an early age, for life in the pioneer settlements of the Carolina frontier was one of constant work and struggle. There was always firewood to cut and land to clear; there were rails to split, gardens to cultivate, orchards to prune, houses to be built and kept in good repair, and a thousand and one other daily chores essential to the maintenance and success of the farm life.

Still, growing up in that comparatively wild and unspoiled land was not all work. All about one was the free beauty of nature, the woods to explore, the creeks to fish, the game to be shot and trapped. Both Mark and Moses, being close because of the short span of years that separated them, loved to go off for a few hours of fishing and to drop their lines in the nearby creek in the hope of snagging a catfish for breakfast or supper. This peaceful pastime re-mained one of the pleasantest memories of their youth. In later years, Mr. George W. Bary, a friend of Moses in Cali-fornia, recalls in a letter hearing the brothers reminisce on this boyhood sport: "Mark and Moses got to talking about the old place and Mark said, 'I wish I had a mess of catfish out of old Crow Creek!' Moses said, 'They are better than these we have here . . .' He (Moses) used to talk about the old stone fireplace and how they went fishing in Crow Creek, and how much better the fish were in Crow Creek than in the sloughs here. He said Crow Creek was a running stream. He never said much about the family, only that they had a large family."*

So there was work and there was play in the western settlements of North Carolina, and sometimes there was formal education. In the 1820's, of course, there was little provision for such. Crude one-room school houses were scattered here and there and whenever a teacher could be secured, sessions in the rudiments of the three R's were held. At best, the education available to most children in the pioneer regions were strictly elementary. Such children were fortunate if they could learn to write their own names, spell out a few lines of newspaper stories or Bible verses, and add a column of figures. In fact, the number of literate persons in North Carolina at that time was so limited that the sanction known as "the benefit of Clergy" was granted to

* Letter to Norman L. Freeman, June 2, 1929.

anyone who could read, write, and quote a few Bible verses. This ancient practice, dating from the Middle Ages, when only the members of the clergy could read and were familiar with the Bible, stated that if a person accused of a crime could prove himself literate before a court of law, he was to be treated as a clergyman and if charged with a crime could be tried only in a church court. The courts of North Carolina continued to recognize this "benefit of Clergy" until late in the nineteenth century, chiefly to encourage citizens to learn to read and write and thus enjoy this special privilege and legal consideration.

The children of the Hopkins family were particularly fortunate in regard to their formal education. Both parents were cultivated persons with a far-above average amount of learning, and both were anxious to pass their knowledge along to their children. All their children, boys and girls alike, were taught by their parents to read and to write. All were able to read from the family Bible and to quote long passages of scripture. It seems that Moses was a particularly apt pupil, and his brothers and sisters were in the habit of making fun of his intellectual conceit and of scoffing at him for his pride in his penmanship. Mrs. Hopkins, however, didn't join her children in this game. She was proud of any child of hers who could write a good hand, read easily, and have a good knowledge of the Bible. She was not only a cultivated woman, but also a deeply religious one and hence was most anxious that her children learn the ways of God and listen to his message in the Bible.

As youth passed and manhood was reached, it became evident to Mark Hopkins that if he was to advance in life he would have to find other means of livelihood than the family farm. There were too few opportunities for personal advancement in farming and the young man yearned for a more challenging way of life. Yet he was deeply attached to his home and family and didn't look forward to the day when he would have to leave all the scenes and loved ones of his childhood. He wanted to adventure into new paths, yet hesitated to leave his aging parents. By the time he had become a young man, his older brothers and sisters had married and were rearing families of their own. His parents were getting less and less able to manage the farm on their own. Most important, his younger brother Moses was becoming a particularly serious problem. And, finally, there was a young woman in the neighborhood whom Mark had admired for many years and hoped someday to marry. He knew he must keep close to home in order to help his parents, watch after "reckless Moses," and be close to the young lady of his choice.

Mark looked about him for a source of income and a way of making a living that would not take him too far from his home. Not far from Crow Creek, on the slopes of the neighboring mountains, was a small gold mine known as the Russell Mine, and here Mark presented himself one day, hoping to learn a new trade and to earn enough money to marry his sweetheart, Elizabeth Jordan. The Russells were well acquainted with the Hopkins family. Several of their sons had married into the family and thus they were glad to accept Mark's offer to join their enterprise.

Mining, particularly gold mining, during the first half of the nineteenth century in the frontier country was a slow, painstaking, and laborious procedure. It was strikingly similar to the methods that were to be used later during the gold rush of the 1850's. In general the method known as "washing" was used, and though this removal of gold from the rocks of North Carolina was not likely to yield millions of dollars' worth of dust or to reveal the nuggets found in the Sierra Nevada mines a decade later, the Russell mine produced enough of the precious metal to provide for the families concerned. For a number of years Mark Hopkins worked in the mines and there learned the practical aspects of mining, came to realize the many problems associated with running a business, and began to develop those talents that were later to prove so invaluable to the transcontinental railroad organization. Engineering, transportation, finance, management—all were involved in the successful operation of the Russell Mines. In later years when he entered the hardware business and then the transportation business, he was able to apply these early lessons to the more complicated operations of his major enterprises.

These years in the hills of North Carolina obviously meant a great deal to Mark Hopkins, for he returned to North Carolina shortly before his death and made a special point at that time of visiting the scenes of his early labors. Blanche Freeman, testifying in the Superior Court of North Carolina, made the following statement:

Q. Did you ever see Mark Hopkins?
A. Yes, sir, in the year 1877.
Q. Did you talk with him?
A. I didn't talk with him much myself; I was a child and he talked to me as a child, but I heard him talk to my grand-

parents (Annie Hopkins) and to my father and mother. He spoke to them about his business. He spoke of what he had done in the gold mine business. He was at my grandfather's (Eli Russell) at that time, who was operating a gold mine. He told what a success he had made as a goldminer. Then he spoke of his railroad business; he had an extensive railroad business; at that time. He spoke of that . . . He went to the Russell Gold Mine.

Q. He was familiar before he left here with the Russell Mine?
A. Yes, sir. He had worked there.

Mark Hopkins' interest in mines and the engineering problems of mining extended to other such enterprises in his home state of North Carolina. During the same 1877 visit he is known to have looked at a second mine in the region. Mr. M. C. Elam, also testifying in the Superior Court of Randolph County, North Carolina, told of his meeting Mark Hopkins at Gold Hill:

Q. Where were you in the year 1877?
A. Gold Hill.
Q. What were you doing there?
A. Running log rockers, washing gold.
Q. Do you remember a man coming there, a stranger to you, at any time?
A. Yes, sir; Mr. Mark Hopkins came there from California; said he had been visiting his brothers and sisters and he stopped in there to see the Gold Hill mine. He said they were washing gold out in California. Mr. Mauney asked him if he didn't want to take stock in old Gold Hill. He said no, he reckoned not. He said they had grit out there, ran anywhere from two feet to 180 feet in the valley. He said they had as good a thing as they wanted out there in California.

Q. Did he tell you about how much gold they washed per week?

A. He said in a week's time they washed out about a ten-gallon kegful of nugget gold.

Q. Did you hear him say what he was doing there?

A. He said they owned stock in railroads and some iron and he said he had come home to see his brothers and sisters on Crow Creek, Randolph County . . ."

A second witness, E. L. Hardister, substantiated Mr. Elam's account of this visit to the Gold Hill Mine when he testified: "The time Mr. Elam spoke about his being at Gold Hill, I carried him (Mark Hopkins) in my buggy. I was carrying the mail at that time."

Thus we know that by the time Mark Hopkins was thirty years old his future seemed fairly certain. He would marry Elizabeth Jordan, a yellow-haired, sweet, and loving girl of the valley, several years his junior, whom he had loved for many years and from whom he had received assurances of affection and loyalty. Already Elizabeth had been welcomed into the Hopkins family and was loved as a daughter and a sister by Mark's mother and sisters. Meanwhile, his earnings at the Russell Gold Mine were increasing year by year so that he could anticipate enough steady income to support a family. As soon as Mark's help at the family homestead was no longer required he could be free to marry Elizabeth. There was only one cloud on the bright horizon, and that was his reckless, irresponsible, rebellious brother Moses. Difficult and troublesome as he was, he still called forth a warm brotherly loyalty from Mark.

It is difficult to understand why Moses Hopkins, of all

the children in the family, was the only one to bring any sort of moral censure and public disgrace upon the Hopkins family. Even as a teen-age boy he had caused trouble in the community and had strained family affection by drinking too freely the local "corn" whiskey. Everyone knew of his inordinate and unbalanced fondness for alcoholic stimulants, and before he had reached voting age his neighbors called him what he was—a drunkard. Accompanying this alcoholism was an innate weakness in moral fiber. He was notoriously irresponsible, disregarded the property and right of others, including his family, and seemed to care little for the opinions of others. He went his reckless way alone. Where others labored for the goods of the world, Moses stole. Where others met their moral and financial obligations, Moses escaped them by fleeing.

The Hopkins family had always worked hard for what they wanted. Hannah and Ned had married and reared a large family. In spite of parental protests and the physical difficulties of the frontier environment, they had succeeded in building a home and a family. In turn, their many offspring had married the partners of their choice and had labored together to make their marriages successful and productive ones, had reared happy, strong, and independent children, and had fulfilled the obligations as citizens. Despite their large number, the family was a closely knit one. Each member knew of the achievements and disappointments of the other; each member was loyal and considerate of the others. Only Moses was outside this functioning unit. He was the "black sheep," the thorn in the side of his parents and brothers and sisters. He defied his family's efforts to help him and to save him from a wretched life. Gone for many months at a time, he would return to the Hopkins homestead only in times of desperate need and poverty. Such a son was surely unique in the Hopkins family.

A modern psychologist might be able to explain why Moses was a delinquent and why he defied all the family traditions of loyalty, self-respect, and God-fearing uprightness. This, however, is not the place for such an analysis. It is sufficient to our story to remember that Moses was a weak person, of good intentions, perhaps, but psychologically and emotionally incapable of fulfilling his intentions. Also it is important to remember that all the other Hopkins' felt it their duty to protect him as much as was humanly possible. His outrageous behavior and lamentable acts called forth from one elderly North Carolinian, a Mr. Herring, the following precise comment: "He wasn't worth a damn."

Possibly, Moses' greatest difficulty was his addiction to strong liquor. All his life, despite repeated promises to "never touch a drop again," he continued to resort to whiskey in time of stress. It was perhaps the frequent pleas from his parents and brothers to stay away from the demon liquor which made Moses feel unwanted at home and pushed him into an early marriage. He left home with his young wife and settled in nearby Orange County. But marriage did not eliminate his need for whiskey. His wife took over the task of curing him; but like all the rest, she failed to make him more moderate. Again, Moses left home. In her plight, the young wife turned to parents and to the community for succor. Moses' reputation became worse; he was more than ever a social outcast and more willing to violate the moral and ethical code of his day. Thus we find him marrying another woman and bringing on his head charges of bigamy, as well as non-support and desertion. Meanwhile, in an antagonistic community it was becoming increasingly difficult for him to find employment. He was unable to support himself by farming and soon turned to stealing what he needed. Several times he was charged with petty larceny for taking trace chains, harnesses, and other necessary farm equipment. His family despaired of ever checking the downward course their young son was taking. The rash deed, the deed that society could not overlook, the crime that would steal his fate in North Carolina, was only a few months away.

In the year 1845, Moses Hopkins finally met his fateful destiny. He committed a truly serious crime, one that in the frontier days of American life was more severely punished than murder or other crimes of passion. He stole a horse— the animal that was the mainstay of American frontier life, the animal most difficult, most costly to replace. To steal a horse was not only an offense against the owner, but a state offense as well. Conviction for such a theft carried a death sentence. Knowing the penalty for his act, Moses must have been a desperate or exceedingly foolish man to risk his life for a horse. No doubt he was again fleeing some charge, some irate citizen, some wronged person, and the horse appeared to him to be his only means of escape.

He committed the crime in March, was apprehended, and was duly arraigned before the Superior Court of Orange County for the spring session of 1845. Charges of desertion and bigamy were also brought. There seemed to be nothing

to stop the harsh and final ways of the law. On the morning
of September 12, 1845, Moses T. Hopkins stood before the
court and was indicted on a charge of Grand Larceny in the
state of North Carolina.

The record of the trial and judgment in this case that was
to change so materially and so irrevocably the life and furture
of Moses and his brother Mark may be found in the Orange
County Courthouse at Hillsboro, North Carolina.   In that
unassuming, simple, work-a-day building lies one of the most
essential keys to the mystery of Mark Hopkins, his family,
his fortune, his estate and its settlement.   But until this time
no one has bothered to examine these records, or wanted to;
for here may be found the link between the railroad magnate
and the Hopkins family of North Carolina.   Here we find
at last the reason for the flight to California, for Mark's
reticence about his early life and family.   For more than a
century these records have been lying, forgotten and dusty,
in the files of the courthouse, holding their secrets from all
the world.

The records reveal that the case of the State of North
Carolina vs. Moses T. Hopkins was heard on September
12, 1845, and the following indictment was made:

SEPTEMBER TERM 1845.   THURSDAY MORNING SEPT. 12

STATE	
v.	INDICTMENT GRAND
MOSES T. HOPKINS	LARCENY

The prisoner Moses T. Hopkins, is put to the bar in his own
proper person and it being demanded of him how he will acquit
himself of the charge set forth in the said indictment which

charges upon him Grand Larceny, saith that he is not guilty thereof and for his trial puts himself upon his Country.

Therefore let a jury thereupon here cause by whom the truth of the matter may be the better known whether he be guilty of the Grand Larceny as set forth in the afforesaid indictment or not guilty, the prisoner Moses T. Hopkins, being arraigned is now put to the bar for trial.

A jury of twelve men was selected, sworn, and impaneled. The case was heard. In the course of it Moses made a significant statement, not only in terms of his own destiny but in terms of future events. He asked for a stay of judgment in the following record, now housed in the Orange County Courthouse and carrying his signature:

State of North Carolina
Orange County

Superior Court
Fall Term 1845

THE STATE
v.
MOSES T. HOPKINS

The defendant Moses T. Hopkins maketh oath that he is not ready for his trial at this term of the court, that two of the material witnesses in behalf of the State are persons of infamous character and are wholly unentitled to credit, that they reside in the State of Virginia, that since he has been arrested in this case he has been confined and has not been able to obtain the testimony that he desires to discredit said witnesses, that by the next session of this court he expects to have Col. John Wilson and Col. John Bailey for this purpose above state, and that this affidafit is not made for delay.

Sworn to and subscribed in open court
(Signed) Moses T. Hopkins.

Though this appeal for a delay did not deter the jury from continuing to hear the case and from passing judgment, it is important to us because of the signature it bears. It identifies Moses Hopkins as the brother of the deceased Mark Hopkins, owner of stocks in the Central Pacific Railroad, financier, director, owner of lands and deeds and transit lines, docks, and other transportation facilities. Years later Moses Hopkins swore blood relationship to a Mark Hopkins whom the papers and the official biographies claim to have been born in New York. Yet signatures on documents from Orange County give irrefutable evidence that this same Moses Hopkins was a resident of Orange County, North Carolina, in 1845, and had more than sufficient reason for wanting to leave his residence and keep his home state a secret.

But to continue with the fateful trial. In due time the twelve honest and true jurors found Moses guilty in the following judgment:

The jurors for the State, upon their oath present that Moses T. Hopkins, late of said County, of Orange, on the first day of March in the year of our Lord, one thousand eight hundred and forty five with force and arms in the county afforesaid one mare of the value of fifty shillings of the goods and chattles of one Jeremiah Morris then and there being found, feloniously did steal take and lead way—against the form of the statute in such case made and provided and against the peace and dignity of the state.

Guilty of the charge against him and subject to the death penalty, how then did Moses save himself to become eventually the beneficiary of his brother's estate?

The next document, also housed in the Orange County Courthouse, tells us all we need to know.

THE STATE
v.
MOSES T. HOPKINS

Prisoner Moses T. Hopkins brought to the Bar, to receive his sentence, where upon it is demanded of him whether he has any thing to say for himself, why upon the verdict and premises aforesaid the court should not proceed to judgment and execution against him, who prays for himself the benefit of clergy, which is allowed him, whereupon it is ordered and adjudged by the court that Moses T. Hopkins the prisoner at the bar be taken to the public whipping post and that the sheriff of this County inflict upon his bare back thirty nine lashes and that he be imprisoned thereafter in the jail of said County until Tuesday of November term next of our Court of Pleas and quarter session for the County of Orange and that then the sheriff inflict upon his bare back the other thirty nine lashes upon his bare back and that he then be discharged upon the payment of cost.

Certainly, Hannah Hopkins had not taught her son to write, to read, and to memorize the Bible in order that one day he might claim benefit of clergy for a crime against a neighbor and against the state! Yet it was this early family training that saved Moses' life. He was given his public whipping, bringing shame and disgrace to himself and to his family. Then he was imprisoned to await his second public whipping.

While serving his jail sentence, his family had a chance to think over the terrible consequences of Moses' unstable character and alcoholism; they had the long fall months to grieve for him, to thank God he had not been executed, to plan for his future. Every member of the family felt concerned in this final and terrible disgrace to the honorable name of Hopkins, yet there was little that any of them could do, except perhaps to pray that the punishment, so justly deserved, would serve as a valuable experience to the wayward Moses, that he would return home a new man, able and willing to take up the responsibilities of a mature person. But there was little reason to believe that this would be the case. Hadn't he left a young wife to poverty and want? Hadn't he willfully and illegally taken another spouse when the law was after him on charges of non-support and desertion? How could one believe that such a man would change during a prison term?

All the family could be grateful for was that the "benefit of clergy" provision had saved Moses' life. Yet they knew that such a provision could only work once. If he were caught again in any deed such as horse-stealing, the provision could not save him from certain public hanging. Instead of improving, Moses had become increasingly recalcitrant; nor had the outcast showed perceptible regret or remorse. Even if he managed to come out of a jail a changed person, there were still two outstanding charges against him—desertion and bigamy—for which he could be brought to law.

It was these doleful thoughts, these inevitable conclusions which ran through Mark's heart and brain during the fall of 1845. He was closer to Moses than were any of the other members of the Hopkins family, and perhaps he knew the personality of his brother best and could appreciate some of the qualities hidden from the world under a cloud of alcohol. Finally, Mark revealed to his family, particularly to his mother, the decision he had reached.

Moses' only hope for a decent life, according to Mark, was to leave the countryside of his birth, the land where all his deeds were known, where he could never shake off public suspicion and antagonism.   Moses must get into a completely new environment where new friends and new opportunities might help him to mend his ways and become a respectful, self-supporting member of society.   In was downright dangerous for him to continue in North Carolina. In his present arrogant, heedless state of mind, there was no way of predicting the way he would behave when he was released from jail.   No one could deny the very real possibility of a new crime when Moses gained his freedom.   How much better then to forestall such a calamity by removing the culprit from the scenes of his former crimes, establish him in a fresh and unaware community, and give him a last chance to prove himself worthy of the name of Hopkins.   It would be necessary for Moses to break all ties with the past—even his beloved family ties.   He and the others in the family must pretend that he was never a member of the Hopkins family of North Carolina.   Only in this way could the man's sorry life be saved; only in this way could the Hopkins' family name be rescued from public censure.

Sad as such a decision was, the mourning mother and the other members of the family agreed that somehow Moses must get out of North Carolina, the sooner the better.   Still, they questioned how successful Moses would be in a new environment.   Wouldn't he repeat the mistakes of the past, piling up enough crimes to warrant the death sentence in yet another state?   To these questions Mark had a ready answer.   The only sure provision against Moses committing new crimes was to provide him with a friend, a friend whom he trusted and respected, who would travel with him to the new territory. Such a friend would be forgiving of his slips and errors, would be a comfort and guide to him in times of temptation. A true friend would guard his secret, protect him against further misfortune, and help him gain self-respect and independence.

Hannah Hopkins could see the reason in Mark's thinking, but though she racked her brain for a person answering to Mark's description, she could thing of no one who was free to take on such a major responsibility. Who would want to save her son from sure destruction? There was no one to whom to go with such a request. Surely, there were many who would want to set out for new lands and new opportunities, but among Moses' friends there was no one qualified for the serious job of rehabilitation. And here we can imagine the good, the serious, the loving Mark turning to his mother and with gentleness and firmness saying to her:

"Maybe there is no such friend," he said, "but there is a person who can save Moses and that is a brother who loves him and understands his shortcomings. There is only one brother free to take on the task and it is I. I have no family, no children—nothing, in short, to keep me here. Therefore as soon as Moses has recovered from his whipping, I shall get him out of jail and together we will set out for those new lands of the West where nobody will know us and where there are ample opportunities for a new and prosperous life. I am the only one free to go with Moses."

Thus it was determined by the family group that Moses should be helped out of jail and that he and Mark should set out for the West. Such a venture was not unorthodox. Many young men were leaving their homes and families for adventure and fortune in the West. Here there were new, virgin, rich soils; here there were forests and plains; here wild animals, abundant fish; here were chances for fortune and fame. The world was changing and America was expanding. Young men of strength and lively spirits were anxious to participate in these expansive times.

But Mark was really not such a person. Thoughtful of his future, enterprising and energetic, yes; but not restless, not in need of new faces and new places. After all, he had his work in the mines, his loving family, and, most of all, the affection of a good woman who had promised to become his wife. It was not easy for him to leave all these comforts and securities for a new land of unknown adventures and hardships. Yet he knew, too, that only he could give Moses his last chance to build a new life. He could only tell his mother and Elizabeth Jordan that he would be back some day, that as soon as Moses had found a new home and new opportunities, he would come back to North Carolina, settle down, and marry Elizabeth Jordon. And so it was determined.

How Moses got out of jail we do not know. We know that most such jails were easy enough to break out of with the help of an intelligent accomplice. We can only surmise that it was Mark who helped him escape. We do know that early in December of 1845 Mark and Moses Hopkins bade goodby to their parents and their brothers and sisters and started out on their long trek westward. A cousin from Orange County, Samuel Hopkins, accompanied the brothers as they left their family home for the last time at two o'clock one windy morning. It had been decided that the three should slip away under the cover of darkness so that none should know where or with whom Moses had disappeared. A new life was starting for Moses and the break with his old one had to be sharp and absolute. More important, if the authorities ever caught up with him, he could promptly and without any legal procedure be brought back to North Carolina to finish out his sentence and to answer for the charges of desertion and bigamy.

An intimate friend of Mark's a John Little, lent him a sum of money to finance the journey. Father Hopkins and Brother John had given each of the men a horse to facilitate their travel. With the love and kisses of the family the three left Randolph County and headed for Kentucky. It was no easy journey. The trails were rough and badly marked; the mountains were steep and rocky; the streams were swollen; the Cherokee Indians dangerous to small bands of travelers. Eventually the three reached the homestead of their Grand Uncle Marcus in Kentucky, and here Mark and Moses decided to stay for a while. Samuel, the cousin, returned to North Carolina, on the weary horse he had borrowed, bringing word to the family of the trip through the Great Smoky Mountains. It was many years before the Hopkins family heard from the two brothers.

For the next few years Mark and Moses remained with their kin folk in Kentucky. But here life was a continual round of arduous chores, with little reward at the end of a

long day of toil. Mark, much as he loved the mountains
and the meadows of Kentucky, wanted to accomplish more
than he could hope to achieve by rough manual labor. He
believed in himself and thought himself capable of achieving
great things, particularly in the line of business. He was
an ambitious, determined, talented person; but the farms
of Kentucky gave him little outlet for his energies and his
experience. While his discontent was growing, the news
of the discovery of gold at Sutter's Mill in California reached
the hills of Kentucky.

The news was further substantiated when some months
later, in the early part of 1849, the two brothers received
a letter from their nephew, James Hopkins. He had gone
out to California over the overland trails in 1845 and had
established himself in Yuma County, California. He wrote
to his uncles of the great changes that were occurring as
a result of the discovery of gold, of the fortunes that were
to be made just for the digging. He urged them to join
him in the foothills of the Sierra Nevada Mountains and
there mine gold with him on his claim.

The letter proved to be the incentive that Mark had been
waiting for. He was fired with the desire to proceed west
and to try his hand at gold mining. He had had valuable
experience at the Russell Mine and was convinced that if
he could get to California he could put this experience to
good use. Moses, who was still restless and unsettled, readily agreed that they should try their luck in the Pacific gold
fields. As far as he was concerned, the farther he went from
the scenes of his past life, the better for him.

But California was a long way from Kentucky. It took money, fortitude, intelligence to make the long trek across the continent. The brothers debated what route to take—the overland trails or the boat trip through the Gulf of Mexico and the Isthmus of Panama. Remembering their comparatively short yet very difficult trek over the mountains from North Carolina, they decided against the overland trails. Their relatives gave them what money they could, and the two started out again, working their way slowly down to the Gulf of Mexico.

Since no letters remain, it is impossible to know the exact route they took. But it seems likely that Mark and Moses first headed for one of the Mississippi River port towns. They there took a steamer to New Orleans, or perhaps they worked for their passage on a flat boat—common enough in those days. From the Gulf they took a boat to Panama and from there another ship up the coast. The Pacific Mail Steamship Company, which had been organized in 1848 for the exact purpose of transporting passengers and goods to the newly-opened gold fields, was at first a subsidized transportation facility, but later, when passengers and goods became abundant, it no longer needed government support and by 1851 it was a flourishing enterprise. Some eleven steamers varying in size from 600 to 150 tons operated between San Francisco and Panama, and it was on one of these, *The Columbus*, that Mark and Moses Hopkins made the last lap of their long journey.

Finally, on May 24, 1851, the Hopkins brothers set foot on California soil when their ship docked at San Francisco. The San Francisco *Daily Alta* on that date listed the 250 passengers which had landed in California from *The Co-lumbus*. Among those names can be found the names of Mark and Moses Hopkins, of North Carolina. This arrival date is of great significance, for in addition to telling us something of the years which had intervened between Moses' crime and the arrival in San Francisco, it definitively prevents Mark from having been eligible for membership in the Society of California Pioneers. This society, which later claimed a Mark Hopkins as a member and wrote a lengthy obituary, had as one of its strictest rules the exclusion of any pioneer who had arrived in California after 1849. The Mark Hopkins of North Carolina did not arrive in the Golden State until 1851.

On that eventful day in May, Mark Hopkins was full of excitement and happy expectations. He felt that here in the far West he could make his real destiny, but he could not have known that here he would become one of the most illustrious builders of California and one of the best-known citizens of his new state.

4

A GENTLEMAN FROM THE NORTH

During the years that Hannah and Ned Hopkins were rearing a family and maintaining a homestead in the frontier regions of North Carolina, another family with the same name was establishing itself in the northern half of the United States. Neither family knew of the existence of the other, and naturally neither could forsee the time when their sons would meet in the then uninhabited regions of the Pacific Coast and there work together in varying capacities toward the building of a vast railroad line linking the East and the West. Yet these two families had some points in common and it was not so fantastic that eventually they should find themselves united in a common project.

Even as the Hopkins family of North Carolina had come from the British Isles, so the northern family had come. However, the northern Hopkins family had immigrated to the new world about 150 years earlier than the southern family and had thus participated in the first colonial settlements. There is no genealogical evidence to indicate that the two families were even distantly related.

The founder of the Hopkins family of the North was a John Hopkins who left England in 1634 and settled in the New England colony. First he went to Cambridge, Massachusetts, becoming a member of Thomas Hooker's congregation at Newtown. Later, when Hooker and his followers tired of the tyrannical ways of the Boston oligarchy and received permission from the General Court of Massachusetts to move into the Connecticut Valley, John Hopkins moved with the group in 1635. He was one of the first to follow Hooker into the new settlement and he is now recognized as one of the original proprietors of the city of Hartford, which was settled by the Hooker group.

From the John Hopkins unit came many more members of the clan. This family continued to live out its days in New England, participating in the many turbulent periods of our Colonial and Revolutionary periods, and contributing their energies, their talents, their labors to the growth of the New England colonies and states. Genealogical records reveal that John's son, Stephen, married a Dorcas Bronson and that in turn their son, John, married Hannah Strong. To this latter couple was born a son, Timothy, who, growing up and prospering, married Mary Judd. From this couple came a son, Samuel, who married Joanna Ingersoll. It was their son, Moses, born on March 13, 1751, at Great Barrington, who eventually became the grandfather of the Mark Hopkins who traveled out to California. Moses Hopkins of Great Barrington lived in his native city and there married Anna Whiting. He operated a general merchandise store and it was in the beautiful Berkshire region of Massachusetts that their son, Mark, was born.

Mark Hopkins, father of the California immigrant, grew up in Great Barrington as had his father, and like his father, he too worked in the family store after completing his elementary education. Here he married Anastasia Lukins Kellogg, a local girl, and the two young people established their first home in Great Barrington just after the turn of the century. During 1801 their first son, Augustus, was born. On September 15, 1803, their second son was born and christened Samuel Frederick Hopkins. After the birth of a third child, a daughter, Mark Hopkins and his wife found themselves getting restless and anxious to move into new country. Thus the young couple, seeking greater independence and larger opportunities, left their birthplace and moved west into upper New York State. The family traveled along the Mohawk trail and eventually reached Henderson, a frontier community in Jefferson County, New York, located along the northeastern shores of Lake Ontario.

Here the Hopkins family settled down, building a new home and establishing a general store in the growing community. This was a large family. In all there were six sons, four of whom lived to maturity, and two daughters. Henry Kellogg, the third son, was born on June 15, 1807, and William, the fourth son, on September 18, 1811. William lived only to the age of eleven, dying of a childhood disease on January 31, 1822. Five years before, his eldest brother, Augustus, had died on August 20, 1817, at the age of sixteen and had been buried in the family plot at Great Barrington. A fifth son, Mark, Jr., was born on September 1, 1813, a year before another baby of the same name was born into another Hopkins family living in Virginia. Following the birth of another daughter, the sixth and last son was born at Henderson on September 22, 1821. He was christened Ezra Augustus in memory of the older brother whom he never knew.

In the city of Henderson the Hopkins family grew up, enjoying the forests in the immediate environs, swimming in the lake and nearby streams, fishing and boating. In the winter, though the air was cold and the ground blanketed with snow, there were skating and sledding to keep a boy occupied when not attending school or shovelling snow from the front of the store and home. When the war of 1812 broke out, this family was, of course, staunchly American in their loyalties and there is no question but what they joined with others in the community to guard Henderson Harbor, on the lake, from British attempts to reach the mainland from Horse Island in the Bay.

In 1820, when Mark, Jr. was seven years old, a census taker for the United States government appeared at his home in Henderson to take an accounting of the members of the Hopkins family. This family data is still preserved in the United States Bureau of the Census in Washington and for the year 1820 gives the following material:

It declared that Mark Hopkins, Sr. had two sons under ten years of age (William and Mark, Jr.), one son between ten and fifteen years of age (Henry Kellogg), one son sixteen to twenty-five years of age (Samuel Frederick), one daughter under ten years, and one daughter between sixteen and twenty-five. His wife, who managed the home herself, was between twenty-six and forty-four years of age, as was Mr. Hopkins, the head of the family.

Five years later, another census taker appeared, this time for the purpose of taking a military count for the State of

New York. This record is also preserved, in the County Clerk's Office of Jefferson County, and it reveals the same basic family data as the 1820 census. The military record states that Mark Hopkins had a family of eight persons, including the head of the house. Of these there were two males between the ages of eighteen and forty-five who were thus subject to military duty, namely Mark, Sr., and son, Samuel Frederick. The other males—Henry, Mark, Jr., and Ezra Augustus—were under eighteen years of age. There were three females in the Hopkins family, one under ten, another between sixteen and twenty-five, and a third between sixteen and forty-four.

In developing our thesis of the existence of two Mark Hopkins' in California at the same time, we rely very heavily on these two census reports, since they establish irrefutably the existence of a New York State Mark Hopkins family and reveal the marked difference between the genealogy as later given out by Timothy Hopkins in the California Courts and the facts as they appear in the Census Reports. Whereas Timothy Hopkins declared under oath that Mark Hopkins, Sr. had six sons, the United States Census Record of 1820 reveals the existence of only four living sons in the Hopkins family. These sons were Samuel Frederick, Henry Kellogg, Mark, Jr., and William. In the intervening five years between the two census reports, one son, William, had died, and another, Ezra Augustus, had been born. The first Augustus had been buried years before. Thus in 1825 the Hopkins family consisted of but four sons. There was no son by the name of Moses; yet Timothy Hopkins, who had already shown his ignorance of the true nature of the

Hopkins family, declared that the New York Hopkins family had a son by the name of Moses. It was his evidence which was accepted in court at a time when the existence of the Census reports was unknown or at least not consulted.

In the latter part of 1825 it is known that Mark Hopkins, Sr. made an important decision—to leave Henderson for new fields of enterprise. The completion of the Erie Canal in that year was a singularly important event. It made it comparatively easy for Easterners to travel into the Great Lakes territories, and again there was an upsurge in the more or less constant drive of Americans to keep moving westward. Mark, Sr. and his family sold the family store, packed the household goods, and joined the move to the Middle-west. Since they left in the last months of 1825, the family must have been among the first to travel down the new Erie Canal. With their trunks of clothing and boxes of goods and household furnishings, the typical American family arrived at Buffalo, the bustling little community that was to become the transportation break in the great east-west route, its warehouses bulging with east-bound farm products and west-bound manufactured goods, its streets and hotels crowded with hundreds of emigrants who arrived daily.

From Buffalo the Hopkins family moved on across Lake Erie to one of the ports along the Lake. Then up the St. Clair river they traveled until they reached St. Clair, Michigan. Here the family settled down to begin a new life. A landscape not unlike that of upper New York State made them feel at home. Here the same need for a general store led Mark, Sr. to open such an establishment and to prosper by so doing. In a short time he came to be respected as a

good citizen and honest merchant.   As a result of his intelligence and sense of fairness he was elected the first probate
judge in St. Clair.   In addition, he performed the duties of
postmaster, administering the local post office in his general
store.   His younger sons and youngest daughter attended the
first schools of St. Clair and his elder sons helped in the
family enterprise.   With a wife in good health, a business
that was prospering, healthy and happy children about him,
Mark, Sr. had reason to feel contented with his marriage
and his move to the West.   For three years he lived with his
family in the growing community and then suddenly in 1828
he died.

The unexpected, early death of Mark, Sr. made all the
rest of the family suddenly aware of their responsibilities.
Even young Mark, Jr. realized that his period of youthful
pleasures and careless joys were over.   Absorbed in his school
work and the outdoor life with his friends in St. Clair, Mark,
Jr. had never thought much about his future.   True, he had
occasionally helped his father in the store, running errands
after school or assisting in the inevitable rush on Saturdays.
Suddenly the death of his father broke this complacency and
disturbed his assurance that all would be well in the future.
When he was fifteen, Mark left high school and went to
work as a clerk in his father's store, now being operated
by his older brothers.

The United States Census of 1830 records that a widow,
Mrs. Mark Hopkins, Sr., lived in St. Clair with her four
sons and two daughters.

Clerking at the family store taught Mark the principles
of business, of keeping accounts, satisfying customers' needs,

ordering supplies and stock. His brothers and sisters did more or less the same thing. In the meantime the mother had died and Henry had assumed the role of head of the Hopkins family. The next United States Census, that of 1840, records that Henry Kellogg Hopkins had married and established a family in St. Clair, that in his household there were four males, one under five, his own son, and three between the ages of twenty and forty, that is, himself and his two younger brothers, Mark and Ezra Augustus. The eldest son of Mark Hopkins, Sr., Samuel Frederick, had by this time left his parental home, married, and established his own household in St. Clair. The 1840 Census also revealed the existence of a daughter under five in Henry Kellogg Hopkins' family, a wife between the ages of twenty and thirty, and a young sister between the ages of ten and twenty.

Sometime in the 1830's before this census of the Hopkins' family was taken, Mark, Jr. had reached maturity and, realizing the limitations of the family business in St. Clair, had determined to leave his parental environment and make his own way in the world. No doubt he also had his father's restlessness and wanted to see new places and do new things. Accordingly he left St. Clair, traveled to up-state New York, and at Lockport, in Niagara County, settled down to a new life. Lockport was near the western terminal of the Erie Canal and hence an ideal town for trade and commerce. The young Mark associated himself with a man named Hughes, and together the two formed the firm of Hopkins and Hughes, a general store for supplying nearby farmers and westward-bound travelers.

Later, Mark formed a second partnership, Williams & Hopkins, dealing primarily in farm implements. As one of the members of the firm, Mark traveled through Ohio and Illinois selling plows to the newly-arrived frontiersmen. Since the firm was only relatively successful, Mark sold out his share in the business in 1837 and returned to St. Clair to live in his brother Henry's home. Thus we find him recorded as a members of the Hopkins family of St. Clair on the 1840 Census report.

Meanwhile, his brother Henry Kellogg Hopkins, no doubt influenced by his father's experiences as probate judge, had taken up the study of law, while his oldest brother, Samuel Frederick, had assumed chief management of the general store. Henry Kellogg had only a small law practice in St. Clair and by the time Mark returned to the parental home, he had already decided to further his law business by moving to a larger city. Mark told him of Lockport and its expanding economy and its significant position on the east-west highway. Accordingly, Henry Kellogg Hopkins closed his home in St. Clair and established his family and his law office at Lockport. Mark, Jr. accompanied him to the New York State community and there studied law with the hope of one day becoming a partner with his brother. While studying law, he practiced in his brother's office. Still, he did not find the law fully satisfactory. On April 18, 1846, Henry died. Mark then gave up the idea of becoming an attorney and took a position as bookkeeper with the commission merchants, James Rowland & Company, located in New York City.

In the big city Mark prospered. He fulfilled his accounting duties so well that in several years he was promoted to the position of manager of the firm. This was a responsible position and a good one; still Mark realized that he could progress no further in the company and would never be able to buy into the old firm. He wanted to achieve wealth and importance, and in the firm of James Rowland & Company he could achieve neither. Still, his nature was one that did not like to take chances or to gamble. New York City was undoubtedly a fine place for a young man to learn the ABC's of commerce, but it was hardly the place for a young man of ambition but without financial or family backing. In the back of his mind was the hope that he could once more establish, perhaps with an equally enterprising young man, a business of his own, where he could expect to reap the entire profits of his labors and talents. He knew the ins and outs of the general store business and wanted to get back into the traditional family occupation.

Just as he was debating these issues in his own mind came the news of gold in the fields of California. It was the incentive for him to move on even as it was the needed push for hundreds of other Americans to take a chance in the West. To these Americans California with its gold nuggets was the El Dorado, the country of wealth and easy riches, the land of opportunity, the place where a man with courage and determination could make his fortune. Mark and many, many others in his circumstances dreamed the bright dream of gold. But while he dreamed, Mark was also practical. He had had no experience with the rough outdoor life of a mining camp, and his character and physical stature were ill suited to the labors and hardships of crude mountain camps. How then could he participate in the wealth of the newly-opened California lands? The answer was easy: in the same way that his father had participated in the wealth of the Middlewest lands—by supplying the miners with the necessary tools, food, and clothing. Miners were just as much in need of supplies as were the farmers who had traded at his father's store.

Thus he decided to go to California. He talked with his cousin, William K. Sherwood; with his brother, Ezra Augustus; and with his old boyhood friends, Edward H. Miller, Jr. They agreed that the three of them could readily leave their homes, since no one of them was attached or had responsibilities to families, and travel to California, there to establish a trading post. One account relates that Mark Hopkins formed a company called the New England Mining Company, twenty-six men joining it by investing 500 dollars each in the venture. With a capital of 13,000 dollars the company bought a large supply of mining equipment, intended for sale in California. With their stock, the three men sailed from New York on the steamship *Pacific*, on January 22, 1849.

Much as these enterprising gentlemen were anxious to take the trip, it was not an easy one. Quarters on ship were crowded, food inadequate, weather conditions treacherous. After the cold of the Atlantic, there were the storms of the tropics, and finally the hazardous passage around Cape Horn. There are plenty of records of travelers by this route to California which reveal the unspeakable conditions on board, the high rates for such accommodations, and the dangers of life at sea. Evidently the *Pacific* was not so bad as some of the other ships making the trip, for we have preserved for us a most unusual note of thanks to the Captain, signed by the hundred of more passengers, for the manner in which the ship made the journey and the way in which they had been treated. This card of thanks was reprinted in the San Francisco *Alta* on August 23, 1849, and reads as follows:

San Francisco, Aug. 10, 1849

To Captain George T. Estabrooks:
Dear Sir—

The undersigned passengers recently arrived on board the ship, *Pacific,* from New York, beg leave to use this method of expressing to you some small degree of the gratitude we owe you for the kindness shown us, on all occasions, during your command of that ship from Rio Janeiro to this port. We assure you we shall ever carry with us a pleasing recollection of a voyage that, though often attended by trials and dangers, has been a source of so much pleasure to us through your humanity and unsurpassed seamanship.

This note was signed by the passengers, among whom were the following: Ezra A. Hopkins, Michigan; E. H. Miller, Jr., W. K. Sherwood, New York; and Mark Hopkins.

Interesting as this note is from the point of view of unusual manners in a usually crude and hurried community, its significance to our story is greater. For here we have another irrefutable fact. The Mark Hopkins of St. Clair, Michigan and of New York State arrived in California shortly before August 10, 1849 accompanied by his brother, his cousin, and his friend, the Miller who later became his business partner

and life-long associate.   It was to be another two years before
the Mark Hopkins of North Carolina and his brother Moses
arrived in the Golden State.   It is indeed fortunate that the
passenger list of 1851, bearing the names of the North
Carolina immigrants, and the thank-you note of 1849, bearing
the name of the Michigan and New York Mark Hopkins,
should have been preserved for examination by historians.
We now have established the existence of two separate, unrelated familities, each with a son named Mark Hopkins, but
only one with a son named Moses.   These sons, having
reached maturity in different sections of the United States,
one in the North, another in the South, determined to seek
their fortunes and their fame in the bountiful El Dorado of
California.   One arrived in 1849, the other in 1851.

In all future revelations and deductions we must now
reckon with the existence of two distinct, separate individuals
whom fraud has made into one personality, doing violence
to the deeds and the lives of both.

5

SACRAMENTO GROWS UP

The capital city of California is today one of America's foremost cities. Its vigorous population, its office buildings and warehouses, its shops and parks, its municipal monuments bear full witness to its rapid growth over a brief span of a hundred years. Yet when Mark Hopkins and his brother Ezra Augustus arrived in the rough and tumble pioneer community in 1849, its appearance held no promise of its future status and quality. In 1849 Sacramento was a disorganized, chaotic community with hastily and poorly constructed shacks, false-front stores, a number of saloons and gambling halls, and a shifting, migrating population that seemed always on the move from or into the town. Clouds of dust rose up each time a wagon or a horse raced down the unpaved streets; or, in the rainy season, the same avenues of commerce would be heavy with mud and water through which pedestrians floundered as they made their way from post office to home or from stage coach to inn. The limited form of government was highly unpredictable and exceedingly subjective. Each man was pretty much a law unto himself; each man was as desirous as the next to make a fortune out of the gold fields with little regard for the property or human rights of others. Gold had made a

54 K. Street and 160 J. Street were devastated by the second Sacramento fire in 1854.

The Great Conflagration at Sacramento, California November 2, 1852.

mockery of the very name Sacramento, bestowed by the Spanish explorer Morago in 1808 in honor of the Holy Sacrament.

Only ten years before the arrival of the Hopkins merchants of New York, the site of the present-day Sacramento had been chosen by Captain John Augustus Sutter, a former Swiss army officer, as the place to establish a New World kingdom of his own. From the Mexican Government, Captain Sutter had received a grant of 50,000 acres of land in exchange for a pledge of allegiance to Mexico. On this extensive area of land he had first built a fort, and soon a prosperous, peaceful, and productive community came into being. Sutter named it new Helvetia in honor of his homeland, using the old form *Helvetia* instead of the modern *Switzerland*. Most of the residents of his community were Indian and Mexican subjects whom Sutter controlled with benevolent but firm hand. His fort served as a trading post for the Rocky Mountain fur traders and often was used as a place of refuge and rest for the first American explorers and settlers who ventured into the Pacific Coast area during the late 1830's and early 1840's. Here Kit Carson, famed Indian scout and guide, and John Fremont, United States Army officer and explorer, were frequent visitors. His fort was a landmark and an oasis in the vast unexplored wilderness of the California lands.

Suddenly into this relatively quiet and controlled existence came the disturbing element of gold. It was Sutter's chief carpenter, a James W. Marshall, who discovered a nugget of gold in the river bed of the California River while he was engaged in constructing a mill on the South Fork of the

American River. The fateful date was January 24, 1848, and it marked a turning point in the whole course of American history. Overnight, as it were, Sutter found his peaceful acres overrun with gold-mad miners. His buildings were destroyed, his cattle stolen, his carefully tended crop fields desecrated, and his employees and subjects lured away under the spell of easy wealth. Sutter's last years were spent in futile efforts to regain title to his property and reimbursement for his losses.

But before this personal calamity had taken place, Sutter had set aside a part of his vast estate for the development of the town of Sacramento. In 1848 the town was planned and in January of 1849 the first lots were sold along the loop of the Sacramento River on what is now Front Street and the lower parts of J and K Streets. In addition, Sutter in December of 1849 gave the new community ten acres of land for a City Cemetery, nucleus of the present Sacramento City Cemetery. When he did this, stores and other places of business had already been established, and here and there were the usual log cabins and adobe homes. Most of these structures were along the river's edge and during the winter floods of 1849-50 they were completely inundated by the swollen waters of the river. Fire soon completed the damage. Flood and fire were to plague and practically destroy Sacramento several times in the ensuing years. Despite these major disasters, the city survived, each time rebuilding with renewed energy.

After their trip up the river from San Francisco, the Hopkins brothers, late of Michigan and New York, reached Sutter's city and found it teeming with gold-hungry men.

Sacramento had become, by virtue of its geographical location, the last stop on the way to the mining camps of the Sierras. It was also the first stop on the way back to civilization and comfort. Here men were busy outfitting themselves for the many months of gold digging or were returning for celebration of their good fortune. Often, too, it was the place where many a weary and discouraged miner ended his days in poverty and despair. But the mood of the city was a cheerful, bustling, infectious one—a mood of chance and sport, of heights and depths. True, lodgings were crude, overcrowded, and too few in number, and many a new resident simply pitched his tent in the city streets or built a shelter for himself out of old packing boxes. Yet the prospect of a fortune made no discomfort unbearable.

Before the Hopkins brothers arrived, the total population in April of 1849 numbered only 110; but by June thousands more had swarmed into the jammed town, and by July a city government of sorts had been formed. In November the population had reached almost 10,000. The business district up J and K Streets and as far as 3rd Street and Front Street had to be extended to take care of the rush of commerce. Daily the boat from San Francisco disembarked more and more men anxious to find their fortunes in the golden hills of California. Along with the miners and the would-be-miners came the Hangers-on—the gamblers, the adventurers, the swindlers, the saloon-keepers, the dance hall proprietors and their hired entertainers, and the misfits and outcasts of the world, each eager to profit in his own way from the newly-discovered wealth of the Pacific Coast. Sacramento grew by leaps and bounds. Even fires

and floods, high prices, poor housing, inadequate food supplies, and lawlessness could not stop the tide of immigrants.
These aspects did not discourage the Hopkins brothers for
whom the primitive conditions of daily living must have
been exceedingly alien and unpleasant.

The Hopkins' and their friend E. H. Miller, Jr. had
arrived in San Francisco on or about August 4, 1849, and
after a week or so in the port city had secured transportation for themselves and their valuable supply of goods to
inland Sacramento. With the sure instincts of a trained
merchant, Mark Hopkins realized that the easiest way to
profit from the newly discovered gold was to exploit men
rather than river beds. It was far easier for a man of his
family background and training to take his gold from the
pockets of miners than from the gullies and creeks of California. His El Dorado was trading, not mining. Everything points to the fact that the New England Mining
Company quickly established its headquarters in Sacramento
and there did a brisk trade in shovels and pick axes brought
round Cape Horn from New York. The flood of that first
winter threatened the supplies as well as the health of the
merchants, but they survived it and by the end of a year
had accumulated a handsome profit from the sale of their
mining equipment. When the stock of the first company
gave out, the firm was disbanded, each member taking his
share of the profits.

Most of the partners in the company caught the gold
fever and set off for the hills to stake out claims in Dutch
Flats of Placerville or Marysville. Hopkins and Miller,
however, decided to resist the temptation to work in the

gold fields and instead maintained their original idea that there was gold in Sacramento in as great quantities as in the mining fields. Combining their profits from the first business enterprise, the two men decided to buy property and to establish their own grocery business in Sacramento. In June of 1850 the firm of Hopkins and Miller was established as a wholesale grocery, and in the fall of that same year the two partners concluded the purchase of a lot at 160 J. St. for the sum of 3000 dollars. There are two significant records of this deed to verify the business and the real estate holding.

The first authentic document is the 1850 United States Census of the city of Sacramento which lists a Mark Hopkins of New York as a merchant, with real estate valued at 1500 dollars. At the same dwelling is listed an Edward H. Miller, also of New York, a merchant, and holder of real estate also valued at 1500 dollars. The second document is the deed book of the County Clerk's Office at Sacramento. Here we note the purchase of Lot Number 4, between 5 and 6 Streets, and running from J. through to K. Street, by Mark Hopkins and E. H. Miller, Jr., from L. A. and F. M. Scott, dated October 19, 1850. The price of the land was 3000 dollars, and the transfer of property was witnessed by B. F. Reed and Mark's brother, Ezra A. Hopkins. These documents demonstrate clearly Mark Hopkins' status as a merchant, as a resident of New York, and as a resident of Sacramento in 1850.

Hopkins and Miller ran a successful grocery and general merchandise store. There were miners to supply, as well as the growing stable population of Sacramento. Mark

Hopkins' experience in his father's stores in Henderson and St. Clair and in his own store at Lockport stood him in good stead, for competition was keen and supplies often difficult to obtain. Miller learned the elements of merchandising quickly and was a capable associate. Both men worked hard and both saved their profits, hoping, of course, one day to be free of the hard work of a merchant. Since vandalism and robbery were prevalent and since lodgings were scarce and expensive, it was good sense for the two men to share living quarters at the rear of the store. The profits that did not go into expanding the business went into the purchase of real estate. The deed records in the Sacramento City Office show that between 1850 and 1852 Mark Hopkins and Edward Miller purchased, sometimes jointly and sometimes individually, numerous parcels of land throughout the growing city. In later years these real estate purchases proved to be of great value and enabled them to gain sizable amounts of money with which to invest in bigger and more lucrative business enterprises.

When the two members of the second Hopkins family arrived in Sacramento, the Mark Hopkins of New York was already an established and prosperous merchant. Like their predecessors, Mark and Moses Hopkins had set foot on California soil at San Francisco and had then taken a boat up the river to the thriving community of Sacramento. Unlike their predecessors, however, they were not interested in the commercial possibilities in the sprawling, unkempt, reckless city; rather, they were like many another immigrant to California who was there to get gold out of the earth. Once more they referred, as they had so many times during

the long voyage to the West, to the tattered letter from
James Hopkins. It told them that James had left his original home in Yuba County (incidently, proof of his residence
there may be found in the 1850 United States Census) and
had moved on to Hangtown, since renamed Placerville,
where he was working a good claim in the dry diggings
there.

Having reached Sacramento, the two brothers were not
far from their final destination. But before setting out on
the fifty-mile trek over sparsely settled countryside, it was
necessary for them to stock up on essential supplies—such
staples as flour and bacon—and to purchase necessary mining
tools. One may even imagine that they used the facilities of
Hopkins and Miller for this purpose. At any rate, they
surely traveled out to the gold region with others on a wagon
train, for it was known to be foolhardy to travel alone
through the lawless and wild Sierra hills. Along the way
they met men returning from the diggings, some with tales
of fabulous discoveries and sudden riches, others with woeful
accounts of empty pockets and empty stomachs. But the
wagon rolled on, the men in it unmindful of the dire warn-
ings, heeding only the lure of gold. At last the sight of
makeshift shacks along the banks of Hangtown Creek and
in the ravines along the valley told the travelers that they
had arrived.

There is no evidence to indicate whether or not the two
Hopkins brothers ever met their nephew. After 1850 there
is no trace of James Hopkins. The fact that he had a claim
and worked a small mine is Placerville is well established,
but no one knows whether or not he was still there in 1851

when the Hopkins brothers arrived. Perhaps he was a victim of one of the bands of outlaws, such as the Owls, who roved the hills around the mining camps, murdering men in their sleep and stealing their precious bags of gold dust. If he were there, it can be readily presumed that the Hopkins brothers joined him in his venture. But even if he was not there, we know that the Hopkins' did at first try their luck in the dry diggings. After all, Mark had had considerable experience in gold mining back at the Russell mine in North Carolina and was confident of success in the mines of California. Though his efforts were not completely futile, still he found the work difficult and the results uncertain. In the dry diggings, water for washing the gold was a major problem and often months had to be spent constructing water runs to a claim. Another method was to pick among the rocks and crevices of the gullies with a long pointed knife, but this, too, was exhausting and often came to naught. After one winter in the Sierras, where the snows were so heavy that mining had to be stopped, and where supplies were small and uncertain, Mark Hopkins realized that mining in California was very different from mining in North Carolina. Then, too, the lawless habits of most of the miners had a bad effect upon Moses who, when his luck was not good, began drinking.

It did not take Mark Hopkins long to realize that the gold of California could be more easily secured from a good, stable business than from the mines. So when the snows melted away in the spring of 1852, Mark Hopkins decided to give up gold mining and to invest his earnings in a grocery business at Placerville.

CERTIFICATE OF MARRIAGE

COPIED FROM LIBER 2 REC. ... 1854

No. of Certificate

Place of Marriage: Borough of **MANHATTAN** No. ___ Avenue/Street

(Groom) **MARK HOPKINS** and (Bride) **ELLEN SHERWOOD**

	Groom		Bride	
Residence				
Age / Color	41	White	36	White
Single/Widowed/Divorced	SINGLE		SINGLE	
Occupation				
Birthplace				
Father's Name				
Mother's Maiden Name				
Number of Marriage				

I hereby certify that the above-named groom and bride were joined in Marriage by me, in accordance with the Laws of the State of New York, in the City of New York, this **20** of **SEPT** **1854**

Signature of person performing the Ceremony **REV. G. SPRING**

Official Station **3 BOND**

Witnesses to the Marriage: ___

Residence ___

BUREAU OF RECORDS   DEPARTMENT OF HEALTH   CITY OF NEW YORK

Top: Marriage Certificate of Mark Hopkins of New York, issued in New York City on Sept. 20, 1854.

Bottom: Preemption Claim signed in San Francisco on Sept. 25, 1854, by Mark Hopkins of North Carolina.

Dates of the two documents are evidence that they could not have pertained to the same man.

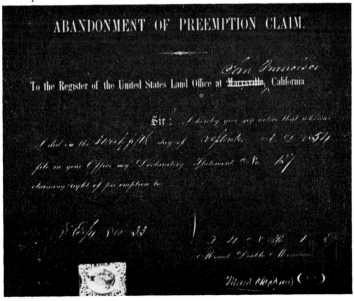

ABANDONMENT OF PREEMPTION CLAIM.

To the Register of the United States Land Office at ~~Marysville~~, California

San Francisco

Sir: I hereby give you notice that whereas I did on the twenty-fifth day of September A. D. 1854 file in your Office my Declaratory Statement No. ___ claiming right of preemption to

STATE OF CALIFORNIA,
SAN JOAQUIN COUNTY.

AFFIDAVIT OF

In the matter of the claim of *Ezra A Hopkins* of *Solano* county,
to the *North East Quarter of*
Section *33*, Township *4 North*, Range *One East*
MOUNT DIABLO BASE AND MERIDIAN.

I, *Moses Hopkins*, of *Solano* county,
California, being duly sworn touching the subject of inquiry, depose and say: I am of lawful age, my
occupation is that of a *Farmer* ; am personally acquainted
with *Ezra A Hopkins* claimant as above; I have known him
about *five* years, or since *185__* I know him
to be a *single* man _ a citizen
of the United States, over twenty-one years of age. I have heard read the above description of the
land sought to be entered by the claimant, *Ezra A Hopkins*, and
know the premises; I know the claimant made a settlement on said land in person, about the ___
day of *July* 185__ that he has inhabited and improved the same, and has erected
a dwelling house upon said premises ___ I know
that he has since lived upon said land and made it his home, and still continues to do so; that the
said land is occupied solely for agriculture and not for trade; it is not enclosed within the limits of
any incorporated town, village or city, and is not within one mile of any military post. I have been
over the said land, and have held conversations in relation to it, and I do not know from my own
personal knowledge, or from hearsay, that there are any SALINES OR MINES OF ANY DE-
SCRIPTION on it, and I verily believe there are none; that the claimant did not quit his residence
on his own land to reside on the public land; and I believe the claimant to be a bona fide pre-emptioner.

Sworn to and subscribed before me upon this
2__ day of *Jany* A. D. 186*3*   *Moses Hopkins*
J S H , REGISTER.

I, *J M Upham* hereby certify that I am personally acquainted
with the above affiant, *Moses Hopkins*, and know him to be a credible
person, a man of respectability, and that full faith and credit should be given to the above affidavit.

Sworn to and subscribed before me this
2__ day of *Jany* A. D. 186*3*   *J M Upham*
J S H , REGISTER.

Moses Hopkins' sworn statement, made in 1863, that Ezra
A. Hopkins was a personal acquaintance—not his brother,
as he later claimed.

After arranging for a lot along the muddy main street of Placerville on which to establish his business, Mark Hopkins returned to Sacramento to purchase the goods for his new venture. Again, he may have turned in at 160 J St. to buy supplies from Hopkins & Miller, for there can be no doubt that the two Hopkins families knew each other during the boom days of Sacramento, as well as later. Buying a wagon load of dry goods and food products, Mark and Moses returned over the slow, winding trail to Placerville and there began business.

Mark Hopkins was not the only American millionaire to get his start in Placerville. Down the street from Hopkins' grocery was Philip D. Armour, later king of the meat-packing business, who at the time was running a small butcher shop. John Studebaker, eventual leader in the automobile industry, had a crude workroom at Placerville where he made wheelbarrows for miners.*

The former farm boy from North Carolina quickly discovered his unusual talents for business and finance. Soon he was enlarging his store and carrying more diversified stock—nails, picks, shovels, and other metal goods in demand among the miners. He made frequent trips into Sacramento to purchase his supplies, leaving Moses in charge of the shop in his absence. But Moses proved to be unreliable and irresponsible. The life of Placerville was too full of drink and lawlessness for the weak Moses. He became more and more engrossed with the unsavory characters of the town, and Mark became increasingly alarmed.

Again Mark had to make an important decision, and again

* *California; a Guide to the Golden State,* New York, 1939, p. 486.

it was necessitated by Moses' unstable personality. Deciding he must get Moses away from the scene of his latest sprees, he went to the store of Hopkins & Miller, a firm with which he had been transacting a major share of his business and one with honest, hard-working proprietors. Mark believed that a job in this firm would keep Moses away from the temptations of Sacramento's "wild life." Thus it was agreed that Moses would clerk in the Hopkins & Miller store and live in the upstairs quarters of the establishment. For a year cr more the arrangement worked very well. Moses seemed to be stimulated by his new environment and challenged by new friends to take a new lease on life. In 1853-54 Moses Hopkins was an employee of the wholesale merchandising firm of Hopkins & Miller. This fact has been gleaned from the Sacramento City Directory for that period.

After the winter of 1853 Mark decided to move his business to Sacramento. Though the city had been subjected to heavy snows and then disastrous floods, and its population had been devastated by an epidemic that followed in the wake of the spring floods, Sacramento was still the boom city of California. It had just been selected as the capital of California; its location on the rivers was considered ideal for commerce; and its opportunities for growth and prosperity seemed unlimited. Placerville, even by 1851, was on the wane and it seemed wise of any businessman to look elsewhere for an investment. To Mark, Sacramento was the obvious choice.

In his search through the city for a likely spot, Mark was assisted not only by his brother, but also by Miller and Hopkins of New York. The latter two knew the city well, were aware of the various real estate offerings and values, and were glad to give suggestions to Mark for his new business, Then, too, the firm of Miller and Hopkins was about to undergo a change in ownership. Mark Hopkins of New York was anxious to bring his youthful sweetheart from the East back to the West as his bride. He planned to buy out his partner and establish his own home and his own business. Miller was agreeable to this, since he was anxious to form a new partnership with his own brother, A. E. Miller. The four men discussed their plans freely with one another and finally reached a conclusion satisfactory to all.

Contrary to all the biographical reports that have yet been published, Mark Hopkins of New York bought out his partner, E. H. Miller, Jr. The deed records of the Sacramento City Clerk's Office state categorically and without any variable interpretation that Mark Hopkins on March 11, 1854, purchased Lot Number 4 at 160 J. Street from Miller and that thereafter this property and the store on it were owned solely by Hopkins. At the same time E. H. Miller, Jr. organized a new firm, known as A. E. Miller & Company, a general store located at 50 K. St.

Not too far down the same block, Mark Hopkins of North Carolina chose a spot for his new business. K. St. in Sacramento was rapidly becoming the important business block of the city, and since it had already been paved with rough planking the year before, it seemed to be the right street for a new business. During his last months of trading at Placerville, Hopkins had been dealing more and more in hardware goods and he felt that he would do better in

Sacramento in the hardware line than in the grocery line. Although another hardware store—Huntington, Massol & Company—was already flourishing at 54 K Street, Hopkins could see from the number of tents and the amount of merchandise that it was doing a booming business and that there was, therefore, room for competition.

Mark of North Carolina spent the spring of 1854 constructing his new store and transferring what stock remained in Placerville to the new site. The structure itself was not much by modern standards. Like its neighbors, the building was in reality a big tent, reinforced with a few wooden posts. Lumber was a very expensive item in those hectic California days, costing sometimes as much as a dollar a foot. The thrifty Mark Hopkins followed the pattern set by other merchants by utilizing tenting and sail material for his shop. By the summer of 1854 Hopkins was beginning to realize a profit for his latest investment of time, money, and initiative. He was ready to think of a time when his store could be well built of strong beams and thick lumber.

Then, on the night of July 13, 1854, all his immediate dreams were shattered. A blaze, said to have originated from a pot of varnish in a workroom behind the Sacramento Hotel on the alley between J and K Streets, flared up, spread to the nearby establishments, and quickly demolished the crude tents and flimsy stores in the vicinity. By the time volunteers could get the flames under control, a good part of K Street lay in ashes, including the new establishment of Mark Hopkins. Though some of the goods were dragged out of the burning structure, the tent, sails, and supporting timbers were destroyed and much of the merchandise was burned and scorched. For the rest of the summer Mark did what he could to repair the damage, but the loss of his supplies was the hardest blow. To all these troubles was added the renewed one of Moses.

Though Mark was discouraged by the sudden turn of events, Moses was completely disheartened. The sight of his labors and dreams going up in smoke knocked all the fighting spirit out of Moses and he despaired of ever succeeding in the business world. He could not be comforted nor sustained, and as usual he turned to whiskey for comfort and release. While Mark was attempting to salvage his business and maintain his relations with his former clients by supplying them with a reduced stock, Moses was spending his earnings in the city's numerous saloons. It was a difficult time for both brothers.

Mark, in desperation, turned to his old business associates, Hopkins and Miller. The Hopkins of the old firm, however, was away. Having broken his business connections with Miller and established his own firm, he had returned to New York to marry his young cousin and would not be back to Sacramento until the following spring. So Mark discussed his problems with E. H. Miller. Among other things, they weighed the possibilities in farming. Mark was discouraged and thought that perhaps he should give up the business world and invest his remaining resources in a farm. There was much to be said for the idea. A farm could always be made to yield a living, however small, and on a farm Moses would be less of a problem. In fact, Moses seemed to find satisfaction out of doors, doing a job where he could see the immediate results. In the country there would be no beer halls, no rowdy companions to stimulate his uncontrollable drinking habit. Then, too, there was plenty of good farmland to be had practically for the asking, since a Congressional homestead act had been passed for California the previous year. Hopkins and Miller talked over the pros and cons of the situation at length. Miller reminded Mark that the younger brother of his former business associate, Ezra Augustus Hopkins, had applied for 160 acres of land in the northeast quarter of Section 33 in Solano County that summer and that he was busy making preparations to settle on his claim. Perhaps he could be of service to the Hopkins brothers.

Ezra Augustus Hopkins and Moses Hopkins had known each other before the summer of 1854 and had always liked each other. With Ezra on a neighboring farm, there was a chance that Moses might be content to work on a homestead claim while Mark carried on the business in Sacramento.

Mark sought out Ezra Augustus Hopkins at the first opportunity and was immediately interested in his description of the fertile acreage that was available for homesteading in nearby Solano County. Moses, too, was interested and the two brothers soon made a trip out to Ezra Augustus' claim. They found his 160-acre claim even more promising than they had expected. There were broad meadows, reminiscent of their grand uncle Marcus' pastures in Kentucky; there was a good woodlot; streams flowed through the area; and the lush vegetation testified to the fertility of the soil. When Mark and Moses learned that the lot immediately adjacent to Ezra Augustus' was still unclaimed, Mark made a quick decision. Immediately on his return from Salano County, he hastened to the nearest United States Land Office and there filed a claim for the south-east quarter of Section 33, Township 4, north of Range Number One East in Solano County. On September 25, 1854, Preemption Claim No. 127 was filed by Mark Hopkins of North Carolina in the United States Land Office. The original records of the old Land Office, now housed in the Department of Interior Archives, show that within two months of each other Ezra Augustus Hopkins and Mark Hopkins filed preemption claims for adjacent sections of land in Solano County, California. Both men knew that within ten years the legal title to the lands would be theirs in exchange for a small sum of money and proof that they had lived on the land, made it into a farm, and improved it with fences, farm buildings, and so forth.

Once he had filed his land claim, Mark Hopkins must have felt easier about the future. Moses showed a real desire to work on the newly acquired property and promised his brother that he would manage the farm by himself. From past experiences, Mark was, of course, dubious of such a quick reform. He strengthened Moses' interest in farming by promising to give up his claim to the land and to allow Moses to take full title if Moses succeeded in running a productive piece of property. The thought of owning his own farm naturally appealed to Moses, but he told his brother not to act in haste. After all, he was still a fugitive from North Carolina justice and was afraid that any document bearing his name might make his whereabouts known. Mark reassured him on this point, stating that as long as Moses kept away from hard liquor and bad company and thus stayed out of the way of any law enforcement officer, his presence in California would be known to no one. He also reassured his brother that the knowledge of his past wrongdoings was a secret shared only by the two of them and that he would continue to keep the crimes a secret to the end of days.

During the fall and winter of 1854, Mark Hopkins divided his time and efforts between Sacramento and Solano County. He continued to operate his reduced hardware store and also gave his time to helping Moses build a small cabin, fence the new land, and clear the land for spring planting. Though the business suffered somewhat by these extra activities, Mark was slowly being recognized as an honest, enterprising, alert businessman. By the spring of 1855 Moses was comfortably established on the farm, the first crops had been planted, and his welfare seemed better secured than ever before. Though Mark loved the country, he enjoyed the gamble and excitement of business more and wanted to move ahead in the mercantile world.

Most of his neighbors on K. Street had suffered almost as much as Mark in the big fire. But perhaps none had taken such a loss as his immediate competitor, Collis P. Huntington. A native of Connecticut, Huntington had arrived in California early in the gold rush and had had considerable success selling all manner of hardware and ironware. He was well known in Sacramento as a sharp and shrewd trader. His business had grown so large that it took five tents to cover his stock, but after the fire, all that had changed. His partners had become discouraged and had sold out to Huntington who was left to manage a recoup of his fortunes as best he could. In the year after the fire, Huntington and Hopkins had come to know each other better and had learned to respect each other's business acumen and skills. Since both were running hardware stores which were suffering for a lack of adequate supplies, it was inevitable that the idea of a combined enterprise should eventually occur to both of them.

On May 1, 1855, the firm of Huntington & Hopkins was officially formed and one of the most famous stores on the West Coast came to life. The firm made a specialty of dealing in mining equipment, and within a few short years nearly every pick and shovel that went up into the mountain mining camps bore the trade mark of Huntington & Hopkins. The firm branched out into a large importing business and soon had expanded into other wholesale markets. It was evident that the two men worked well together and that they each respected the skills of the other. This mutual respect and trust was to show results in the partnership that enabled the Central Pacific Railroad to become one of the nation's major transportation lines and to become a phenomenal financial success. Huntington once remarked of Mark Hopkins: "(He) was the truest and best man that ever lived. He had a keen analytical mind, was thoroughly accurate, and took general supervision of the books, contracts, etc." *

While the Mark Hopkins of the South was busy with the affairs of his brother Moses, with his land claim, and with his new association with Huntington, the life of the Mark Hopkins of New York was undergoing considerable

* F. N. Bancroft, *Chronicles of the Builders*, Vol. 5, p. 40.

change. Shortly after E. H. Miller had sold him his share of the grocery business at 160 J. Street, he had closed his store temporarily in order to make the long six-month journey back to his native state. It was indeed a long trip and a costly one, but the goal seemed worth the effort. He had done well during his four and a half years of merchandising and real estate buying in Sacramento and felt himself in a secure enough financial position to marry his boyhood sweetheart, Mary Frances Sherwood. Mary Frances was the sister of William K. Sherwood who had sailed west from New York on the same boat with Mark Hopkins and E. H. Miller, back in 1849. She was also a cousin of Hopkins. Her family, like his, had originally come from Great Barrington, Massachusetts, where her parents, William and Lydia Sherwood, had lived until 1833. Hopkins reached New York in September, 1854, and the marriage of the two cousins took place several days later in one of the oldest brick churches in New York City.

There are three existing records attesting to this marriage, and it is a curious fact that each document varies slightly from the other, proving once again how carelessly details of such vital statistics were treated even up into the middle of the nineteenth century.

The New York *Herald* for September 22, 1854, carries an item that reads: "In the City of New York on Wednesday, September 20, the Rev. Dr. Spring married Mark Hopkins, Esq. of Sacramento City, California, to Miss Mary Frances Sherwood, daughter of William Sherwood, Esq." In the church where the ceremony took place the record books give two entries on the event: "Mark Hopkins to Sherwood,

Sept. 20, 1854," and "Sherwood to Mark Hopkins, Sept. 20, 1854." It was odd that the Christian name of the bride should have been omitted in both entries, but what is odder still is that the record in the New York City Bureau of Records and Statistics, Department of Health, should read: "Borough of Manhattan, Groom—Mark Hopkins, age 41, white, single; Bride—Ellen Sherwood, age 36, white, single. I hereby certify that the above named groom and bride were joined in marriage by me, in accordance with the Laws of the State of New York, in the City of New York, this 20th day of September 1854. Rev. G. Spring." Obviously the Reverend Spring did not know the couple very well since he omitted the bride's Christian name from his own church accounts and gave her the wrong name in the New York City records. However, it is perfectly clear that Mary Frances Sherwood was married to Mark Hopkins in New York City on September 20, 1854.

This date is most significant, since it is just five days before another Mark Hopkins was filing a preemption claim in a United States Land Office in far-off California. It establishes beyond a shadow of a doubt that there were two persons by the name of Mark Hopkins and that Mary Frances Sherwood married the Mark Hopkins of New York. Later she was to pass as the wife of the Mark Hopkins of North Carolina.

After the marriage the couple left immediately for Sacramento, the long voyage serving them as the wedding trip. Mark was anxious to return to work, for he had been away for almost a year and many changes had taken place during his absence. He had fortunately escaped the catastrophic fire; he had not yet seen his brother Ezra's farm; and he had yet to learn of the new partnership involving his southern friend, Mark Hopkins, and the hardware merchant, Collis Huntington.

Upon arrival in the booming city, Mark Hopkins took his new wife to their home above the grocery store on J. St. and promised her they would soon move into a proper home outside the commercial section of the city. Meanwhile, Mrs. Hopkins helped in the store, serving as clerk when her husband was out on business or scouting around for more real estate. Shortly after his return to Sacramento, Mark Hopkins and Mary Frances Hopkins bought three adjoining lots on M. Street, where they presumably built their home. However, the M. Street address is not listed as a residence until 1865. The deeds to these lots were made out to both Mr. and Mrs. Hopkins, thus complying with the California law requiring the signatures of both husband and wife on property claimed by both of them. This record is another important thread in the tangled Mark Hopkins story. For a title deed to be legal, the law required it to carry the signature of the wife, yet we find that in later years Mrs. Hopkins claimed property bought by the North Carolina Mark Hopkins, the title deed to which carries only his signature. It can be seen then that Mrs. Hopkins was violating the law when she claimed inheritance to land that did not bear her signature, though she stated it had belonged to her husband—a claim completely against the laws and legal traditions of California!

The next six years seemed to be prosperous ones for the Hopkins couple. Their business increased in volume and by 1860 Mark Hopkins was able to report to the United States Census taker that he owned real estate valued at 18,000 dollars and personal property valued at 20,000 dollars. He had bought property outside the immediate limits of the city and on it employed two laborers to run a small truck farm for supplying his store with fresh vegetables. He and his wife made frequent sojourns to Ezra's farm, and Mary Frances often spent the hottest months of the year in the cooler, quieter farmstead. They had no children of their own, but they did have young people in their home. Mark had sent for his nephews from St. Clair, and the oldest son of his brother Samuel Frederick had come to join his uncle. This young man's name was also Mark, so that Sacramento had for a time three Mark Hopkins' among its residents. Though sometimes the names of the three men were confused, there was no confusion in the mind of their neighbors as to which was which. The three were usually distinguished by the nicknames of "Big" Mark, "Little" Mark, and "Young" Mark. These adjectives, obviously, did not refer to relative heights or girths of the men involved, but rather to their status in the business world. "Big" Mark Hopkins of North Carolina was the partner of the flourishing firm of Huntington & Hopkins, rapidly becoming one of the most powerful and best-known importing firms on the West Coast. "Little" Mark Hopkins of Michigan and New York was the grocery merchant; and "Young" Mark Hopkins of St. Clair, Michigan, was his nephew and assistant. These sobriquets became more appropriate with the passing years and as the various Hopkins men entered the railroad business. Again the North Carolina Hopkins

was the "Big" man of the trio in his position on the Board
of Directors and as one of the original founders of the
Central Pacific Railroad. "Little" Mark continued to describe the New York Hopkins who served as one of the
several treasurers of the company; while "Young" Mark
served as a deputy treasurer.

Despite the obvious differences in wealth, position, and
background of the three Mark Hopkins', it is often difficult
to trace their individual careers at particular times. For
instance, in April, 1855, one of them was elected a Council-
man of Sacramento on the ticket of the newly organized
Republican Party. He held this position until April of the
following year. Now much has been made of this fact and
many of the railroad histories mention this election because
Charles Crocker and Leland Stanford were also members
of the Board of Councilmen at the same time. The historians
have felt that the short political tenure of the three men on
the same board established the basis for their later association
in the financing of the Central Pacific Railroad. No doubt,
similar political convictions helped to cement the friendships
of the men, but it must not be forgotten that Huntington,
although he never held a political office was one of the first
staunch supporters of the Republican Party in California.
He and Hopkins donated the use of their storeroom above
their business offices to the newly formed party for its meetings and conferences. They also gave space to the Sacramento *Bee*, the first Republican newspaper in California,
located at 52 K. Street. Hopkins of North Carolina undoubtedly shared his partner's political views and would

therefore have met Stanford and Crocker even if he had not served on the Board of Councilmen.

That as modest and retiring a man as the Southern Hopkins ever ran for a public office appears hard to believe. Not only would his character and his unwillingness to put himself in the public eye mitigate against such a move, but his desire to avoid any publicity for himself in the event that it might attract attention to Moses would also stay any such action on his part. It seems more likely that Mark Hopkins of New York was the one who held the political office. Perhaps it was his nephew, since he was closer to Stanford and Crocker in age, around thirty years old, and had the enthusiasm as well as the Yankee-Middle-west background that would make the tenets and platform of the Republican Party attractive to him.

In the ten years between 1850 and 1860 Sacramento grew from a tiny settlement on Sutter's farm to a city of many thousand inhabitants, boasting both residental and commercial areas, and proud of its choice as Capital of the State of California. As Sacramento thrived and expanded, so did the lives and fortunes of the Mark Hopkins' who had come from the North and from the South. Notwithstanding the histories and the biographies, there is enough documentary evidence to prove that two men, and sometimes three, with precisely the same name lived and worked in these early days of Sacramento.

In the previous chapter it was demonstrated that the New York Mark Hopkins arrived in California some two years before the North Carolina Mark Hopkins did. Some historians, cognizant of the discrepancies in dates, have said

that in 1851 Mark Hopkins returned East and brought his
brother back with him in May, but such a feat would have
been impossible. The trip from San Francisco to New York
in the 1850's took at least five months and usually much
longer. To have made a trip to the East and to have arrived
back in Sacramento again by May 24, 1851, Hopkins would
have had to leave California in August or September of
1850. Yet there is a deed record of the land Mark Hopkins
bought on J. Street and its date is October 19, 1850. No
man at that time could have traveled more than 7000 miles
across the continent and back in a period of eight months.
It is positive, therefore, that the New York Hopkins was
already settled in Sacramento before the Hopkins of North
Carolina stepped on a westbound ship for California.

A second error that constantly appears in the several histories and biographies of the Big Four states that Hopkins
sold out his interest in the grocery business and formed a
new partnership with Collis P. Huntington. This is a
definite confusion of the two men's careers. Again, the deed
books show that Hopkins bought out Miller's share in the
firm of Hopkins & Miller. Both men were established in
separate, individually-owned establishments for a year before the Hopkins of North Carolina arrived on the scene
to form a partnership with Huntington, resulting in the
famous firm of Huntington & Hopkins. E. H. Miller did
not buy out the Hopkins of New York, nor did the grocery
merchant go into a business partnership with Collis P. Huntington. By 1855 none of the three men were associated in
a business way, although as merchants they certainly knew
each other.

The records of the marriage of Mary Frances Sherwood to Mark Hopkins are a third point of clearing up the confusion. These records clearly differentiate between the New York man who returned to New York State to marry and the North Carolina man who at the time was filing a land claim in Solano County, California. Within five days of each other, one Mark Hopkins secured a wife in New York City and the other secured a preemption claim to 160 acres of California land.

Biographies to the contrary, there were two Mark Hopkins, each doing different things in different places at the same time. Government and city records cannot be disputed. They must be used as the basic source material in any biography or in any historical account. These clearly reveal that there was a Mark Hopkins who married a wife named Mary Frances Sherwood in the city of New York. And just as clearly they reveal that there was a Mark Hopkins for whom there is no record of a marriage.

6

RAILS COME TO CALIFORNIA

When the Hopkins brothers arrived in the rough frontier state of California they knew from hard personal experience the woeful inadequacy of transportation to and from the growing, booming community of the Pacific Coast and the settled, comparatively comfortable areas of the East and Middlewest. All the varied means of travel—foot, flat boat, steamer, stage coach, horse and buggy, Conestoga Wagon—could never provide the kind of transportation that was indispensable to the continued growth and prosperity of the West. Though many immigrants had private dreams of fame and fortune, all shared the one dream of a railroad that would link the mining towns to the commercial centers and supply ports and would tie the West to the East. Without such a link, California, for all its natural resources, its mineral deposits, its magnificent coast line, its tall forests, and its courageous inhabitants, could not hope to realize its potentialities.

One Historian has written: "The importance of railroad expansion in American history in the half century after 1860 can hardly be overestimated. Our industrial and agricultural development was dependent upon internal transportation, of which the major part was furnished by the railroad. The very settlement of large sections of the West was promoted by the railroads, built in many instances through unoccupied regions with the settlers following in their wake." *

As an alert, forward-looking resident of Sacramento, and as anxious as other Californians to see his adopted state grow to its present eminence, Mark Hopkins, partner in the firm of Huntington & Hopkins, must have fully recognized the pressing, desperate need for a system of railroads. Only with such a system, linking one mining town to another and helping California become an active and integrated member of the Union, could the commerce, agriculture, and industry of the state bring to the businessmen, the farmers, and the financiers the profits they had come to win in this raw, wild, and uninhabited land. When Hopkins came from North Carolina to the West to find a new life for himself and his brother, he came hoping to share in these profits. Like his fellow citizens of California, he was eager to achieve future personal security and wealth. Obviously development and prosperity were dependent on an efficient, fast transportation system. The only answer for the state and for the individuals in it was a railroad system that would serve the widely scattered towns and cities and would bind with iron rails the Pacific Coast to the rest of the United States. It was not until 1854, however, that their dreams for commercial expansion began to take shape.

In that year, just a few years after Hopkins himself had arrived in Sacramento, there came to the Pacific Coast an energetic, far-sighted, sometimes wild-eyed, but always opti-

* Harold Underwood Faulkner, *American Economic History*, 6th ed., Harper & Brothers, New York, 1949, p. 486.

mistic engineer by the name of Theodore Dehone Judah. A young man of twenty-seven at the time, he had already helped build bridges in Vermont, survey railroad lines for the states of Massachusetts and Connecticut, assist in the construction of one of the sections of the Erie Canal, and execute plans for the building of the Niagara Gorge Railroad, the marvel of the 1840's. Just before coming to California he had been busy with the construction of the Buffalo end of the Erie system of railroad lines. An experienced and gifted engineer, he was the perfect choice of the group of Sacramento businessmen who had just determined to finance a railroad for their community. One of them, C. L. Wilson, president of the group proposing the line, chose Judah for the job. With his wife, Judah left Buffalo and arrived in California in May of 1854. By the end of that month he had completed a preliminary survey for the proposed railroad line which was to run between Sacramento and the placer-mining districts in the foothills of the Sierra mountains. During the winter of 1855 almost a hundred men were employed in the difficult task of grading a road bed between Sacramento and Placerville. In August, 1855, four officials of the Sacramento line were given a hundred yard ride in a car on the newly laid track, becoming the first men to travel on a Pacific Coast railroad. By the end of the summer a locomotive and two flatcars were drawn a distance of fifteen miles; and in the next year, in February of 1856, the first railroad on the California coast was officially completed. Though new settlers poured into Sacramento as a result of this completion, the once prosperous mining towns began to lose their reason for being—receipts from the placer mines fell off, and the railroad that had been expected to spread the length and breadth of California began to fall into disuse. What had once been envisioned as the beginning of a vast network of iron was left to rust away in the ghost towns and valleys of the Sacramento area.

With his work completed for the Sacramento Railroad Company, Judah turned his alert brain to a project much closer to his heart—the building of a rail line that would connect the great state of California to the argicultural and commercial centers of the Middlewest, the East, and the South. Such a project was not an original idea with Judah. For more than two decades, farmers, merchants, builders, and bankers had discussed the feasibility, the cost, the extent, and the route of a transcontinental railroad that would span the broad prairies, the deserts, the mountain ranges, the farm lands, and the forests of the American continent. But in 1855 this dream had many miles to go before it could become a reality. Railroads, even in the eastern areas of the United States, were still a novelty. The first railroad bridge across the Mississippi River had only been completed in that year. More than 2000 miles still separated the East from the West.

One of the earliest men to insist that such a feat was within the realm of possibility was Asa Whitney, a New York merchant who had made a fortune in the China trade. In spite of his pleas to business acquaintances and to members of Congress for sufficient funds to begin such a project, he failed to see his dream come true. Nevertheless, there were others to keep the idea a burning issue. Conventions were held during the years after Whitney's death to stimulate public and private interest in a transcontinental railroad. But limited capital, debate over the route to be used, and the difficulties in connecting such a line with established Eastern railroad lines always prevented these numerous conventions from being anything more than talk sessions.

The first difficulty, the one that remained a constant factor in the later history of the railroads, was the lack of funds. Since railroads had always been considered along with public roads and bridges as a necessary form of public improvement, they were generally financed by the community. But when individuals in the community hesitated to invest their private funds in a public venture, those wanting the rail lines had to look elsewhere for capital, in particular to the Eastern bankers and business men. The procedure was fairly simple. Small governmental units—such as a town, county, or city—would issue bonds to be exchanged for railroad stocks or bonds. Then the town bonds would be sold by the railroad entrepreneurs at large discounts to investors in the East. Sometimes the state governments issued the bonds that were to be exchanged for railroad stocks which could be sold cheaply on the stock markets. Texas, for instance, was quite successful in getting railroads in its area through this expedient. But, in general, the political units were unable to pay off the bond issues and soon it became increasingly difficult for the towns and states to get the necessary credit from wary Easterners.

In the end, it was the federal government, with its greater prestige and larger sources of capital, which financed the bulk of the rail lines throughout the United States, particularly in the West. By 1850 the principle of federal aid to the railroads in the form of extensive grants of land was a firmly established one and one that was used to build all the railroads thereafter. Most of these grants were similar. The railroad company was given alternate sections within a six- to ten-mile radius on either side of the proposed route. This land was then to be sold by the railroad to settlers and investors who would buy the land at auction in the belief that a railroad line near their property would insure increased prosperity and high land values. The revenue from these land sales was to be used as the major capital for building the line. Altogether some 180 million acres of public domain were given to the railroads, with sales from these lands amounting to almost 500 million dollars. On occasion, the federal government gave additional assistance to the railroad entrepreneurs by granting them generous loans on the basis of a mortgage.

A second major impediment to the construction of a transcontinental railroad was sectional disputes as to where the line should run, since nearly every section advocated its area as best suited. All were agreed, however, that the road should end in California. By 1852 the choice had narrowed down to four or five main routes. The first, advocated by Whitney, was the most northerly, following the old wagon trail from Lake Michigan to the Columbia River. Below this route was one proposed by Senator Benton; it would follow the 38th and 39th parallels, start at St. Louis and terminate at San Francisco, crossing the upper reaches of the Rio Grande, and continue west through southern Utah, turning then to cross the Sierra Nevadas into San Joaquin. Yet another route, known as the southern route, would cross the state of Texas to El Paso, follow the Gila River to the

Colorado, and cross the desert to San Diego. These routes—
the northern, the central, and the southern—were the most
favored in the debates that ensued.

In 1852 a Congressional survey directed by Jefferson
Davis, then Secretary of War, showed that four routes were
feasible, each with different advantages. Davis gave his support to the southern route and was thus charged with pro-
slavery and sectional motives. The debates continued. Even
the people of California, motivated by desire for personal
gain, were unable to agree on the route to be followed within
the state. It was the Civil War which forced Congress to
do something to hold the state of California loyal to the
Union and which removed the southern route from the
competition.

Meanwhile, Theodore Judah had maintained his enthusiasm for a transcontinental line and had worked on a number of surveys during the years between 1855 and 1860.
He visited Washington to get support for passage of a bill
giving grants of land to the state of California for railroad
building. He explored the Sierra Nevada mountains for an
adequate wagon road, and he was a delegate to the Pacific
Railroad Convention, where he advocated a thorough survey
before choice of a final route. As the result of a second
trip to Washington he was able to assure all those who would
listen that Congress was psychologically ready for a railroad
grant to anyone who would undertake the increasingly urgent
task of building a transcontinental line. On his way back
from this second Washington visit, Judah surveyed the
canyons and foothills around the town of Dutch Flat in the
Sierras. Here he found a practical route for a line over the

mountains. With his usual infectious enthusiasm he was able to get a pledge of 46,500 dollars from citizens in and around Dutch Flat, and with this contract he rushed on to San Francisco to try to persuade the larger financiers of the big city to make comparable contributions to a company to be known as the Central Pacific Railroad of California.

Turned down by the financiers of San Francisco, he went back to Sacramento and began to organize meetings of businessmen and bankers in that town for the purpose of discussing finances. The first such meeting was at the St. Charles Hotel on K Street, but this was poorly attended and so a second was held, this time in a small room above the hardware store of Huntington & Hopkins. It was natural that these two leaders in the community should play host to the town's merchants. Of the dozen or so citizens there, two others proved to be important in future events—Charles Crocker and Leland Stanford, the first a drygoods dealer, the second a wholesale grocery merchant with political ambitions. To these four men, Judah's description of the wealth that could be gained by controlling the freight and passenger service between Sacramento and the mining fields of Nevada made good sense. At the conclusion of the meeting the four merchants, plus a few others, agreed to finance a preliminary survey of a route running from Sacramento to the Dutch Flats. By June of 1861 a company was organized under the laws of California that was to be known as the Central Pacific Railroad of California. Capital was set at eight and a half million dollars to be obtained by the sale of hundred dollar shares. Huntington, Hopkins, Stanford, and Crocker each subscribed to 150 shares and elected themselves, with Judah, Strong, Bailey, and Marsh, who had also subscribed to the capitalization, the first directors of the infant concern.

In October, 1861, Judah had completed a truly detailed survey of the 115 miles between Sacramento and the eastern boundary of California, following a ridge from the town of Lincoln to the top of the mountains where the route then wound down the side of the mountains along the Truckee River into Humboldt Sink. Today, travelers on the Central Pacific still ride over this original survey route.

With the survey completed and winning the approval of the four chief investors, Judah left for Washington to get government aid in financing and constructing the line. Here, for the first time, Judah met with enthusiasm. The war separating the South from the North was on; the need to hold the far western states within the structure of the Union was urgent; and all could see the desirability of a railroad line that would cement existing feelings of loyalty. With the help of several influential Western congressmen, Judah saw his dream begin to take real shape when in the midsummer of 1862 a bill to assist the construction of a Pacific Railroad was passed and on July 1, 1862, signed by President Lincoln. Two years later a second Pacific Railroad Act was passed to further the original government subsidy. In all, the two acts, accepted by the companies concerned, made the following grants and provisions: First off, the Central Pacific was authorized to complete its first lines from Sacramento to the eastern border of California and to continue to build eastward until it met up with the Union Pacific, which was authorized to extend its lines westward. The Central Pacific was also granted the right to extend its service west and south from Sacramento and San Francisco. A 400-foot wide right-of-way was granted for the actual lines and the stations, offices, and construction units necessary to the operation of the railroad. But the most generous aspect of the laws gave to the merchants of Sacramento, the organizers and founders of the corporation, a grant of ten alternate sections per mile of public domain on both sides of the line along the entire length of the railroad. This was surely one of the most extensive land grants ever made to a private corporation. Further assistance came in the form of a government loan to the two companies involved in the transcontinental venture. In exchange for thirty-year bonds bearing 6 percent interest, the companies were lent so much money per mile, the amount to be determined by the type of terrain crossed by the lines. For level, clear areas the rate was 16,000 dollars a mile; for difficult and mountainous terrain the rate went as high as 48,000 dollars.

Here then was the basic financial structure of the Central Pacific Railroad. Added to it were the numerous municipal, county, the state subscriptions to the stock of the Central Pacific. The four Sacramento merchants, though prosperous enough by local standards, could never have amassed the necessary capital for so gigantic an enterprise. Only through public support could this strictly private corporation have gained its objective. Stuart Daggett, in his important *Chapters on the History of the Southern Pacific*, has written: "Almost half of these assets [those of the Central Pacific Railroad] were derived directly from political bodies of one type or another, and the value of the remainder of those assets was dependent for the most part upon the security which was afforded by the government donations made to the company." *   Nevertheless, the four Sacramento merchants continued to hold complete control of the destiny of the corporation, Huntington acting as financial and purchasing agent, Hopkins handling the complicated treasury work and managing the business, Crocker being in charge of construction, and Stanford being responsible for the delicate political aspects.   These four worked in harmony and with confidence and trust in each other.   Never did the affairs of the corporation slip out of their hands.   From the very beginning, they exerted tremendous executive power, keeping most of their transactions secret and unto themselves, never allowing even government officials to examine their books or records.   By virtue of what seemed at first to be a simple scheme for gaining new trade markets, they became the Big Four of California, ruling the lives and fortunes of thousands, taking untold profits from the chief railroad line as well as from their subsidiary corporations.

Though many economists and historians have tried to unravel the business affairs of the giant corporation, none has succeeded.   One of its operations was the establishment of a construction company, owned and operated by the Big Four and selected by the Board of Directors of the Central Pacific Railroad as the chief firm for building the line.   A historian has summarized this dubious form of financing in the following succinct manner:

The Central Pacific Railroad "was so successful in mud-

* Daggett, *Chapters on the History of the Southern Pacific*, The Ronald Press Company, New York, 1922, p. 25.

dling its accounts no one has since been able to disentangle them. Huntington, Stanford, Crocker, and Hopkins held the capital stock (of the Contract & Finance Company), paying for it with their personal notes. Then in their capacity as controlling stockholders in the Central Pacific they voted themselves lucrative construction contracts. The money for the construction was advanced by each man as he had extra cash, and in every case the only record of the transaction was his own memorandum. Profits were either put back into the business or divided equally. This scheme of bookkeeping had wonderful possibilities in preventing too close inquiry into the company's methods and accounts. The last dramatic bit of confusion was added with the 'accidental' destruction of the company's books by fire in 1873." *

The survey completed, and the method for financing firmly established, the executives, with the aid of their chief engineer, Judah, pushed forward the spanning of a continent. But there was one flaw in the perfect scheme. Judah proved unwilling to accept many of the suggestions of the four financiers, particularly those aimed at making greater profits by questionable deeds. In September, 1863, he broke away from the company, getting, it is said, a mere 100,000 dollars for his shares in the firm. The next month he left California to seek support from Eastern bankers, but on the boat moving through the Isthmus he caught yellow fever and reached New York only to die there a week later, on November 2, 1863. He was not yet thirty-eight when he died. Never did the four directors give him credit for his

* R. E. Riegel, *America Moves West*, Henry Holt and Co., New York, 1947, p. 476.

In Witness Whereof, the said CONTRACT AND FINANCE COMPAN
*has hereunto caused these presents to be signed by its Presiden
and Secretary, and sealed with its corporate seal, the day an
year first above written.*

Mark Hopkins

President, C. & F. Co

W. E. Brown

Secretary, C. & F. Co.

. S. Crocker & Co., Steam Printers and Stationers, 42 and 44 J Street, Sacramento.

Registered signature of Mark Hopkins as President of the
Contract and Finance Company.

role in planning and working for the continental railroad
line. He remained forgotten and neglected until sixty years
after his death when a bust of the great engineer was unveiled at the Sacramento railroad station.

In spite of the loss of their chief engineer, the work of
building the line moved forward. On January 8, 1863, in
the streets of Sacramento the first work on the line was
begun. By September, 1865, in spite of great obstacles in
getting supplies and laborers (many of them Chinese coolies
specifically imported for the purpose) and in spite of
wretched weather conditions, the line extended fifty-six miles
eastward from Sacramento—as far as the Sierra Nevadas.
This formidable barrier was crossed in December of 1876,
at an elevation of 7042 feet, and from there Crocker drove
his work gangs eastward, hoping to outdistance the westward-
moving Union Pacific forces and thus gain greater land
grants and larger government loans. On April 29, 1869,
Crocker and his forces set a world's record in railroad con-

struction when he reported that ten miles and 185 feet of track had been laid that day.

By the early months of 1869 the two teams could see and hear each other, and their lines met at promontory Point, Utah, just west of Ogden. The Central Pacific had built 689 miles of railroad line, the Union Pacific 1086. The formal ceremony marking the meeting of East and West took place on May 10, 1869, a little less than seven years after Abraham Lincoln had signed the first Pacific Railroad Act. The dream of a nation had been realized and to celebrate the great occasion all the notables of both lines were present, together with important political and financial leaders. With the lines joined, there remained only the last spike to be driven. From Arizona came a spike of gold, silver, and iron; from Nevada a spike of silver, and from California the Golden Spike, driven by Stanford of the Central Pacific and Durant of the Union Pacific. As they wielded the sledge that drove the spike into the rails, the locomotives standing by tooted their whistles, heard in the Eastern cities by telegraphic connections. A nation rejoiced. The telegraphic dispatch shouted jubilantly: "The last rail is laid! The last spike is driven! The Pacific Railroad is completed!"

A photograph of this memorable event has been preserved and a painting of it has been stored in the collection of the Wells Fargo Bank. It shows, standing near Stanford and Durant, the small figure of Mark Hopkins, the man who had grown from the pioneer boy of the North Carolina hills, the man who had traveled the breadth of the United States, worked in the gold mines of California, labored in homesteading and store-keeping, the man with the special vision to gamble on an engineer's wild dreams. His future was assured. As a director of the great corporation which had accomplished half of this magnificent deed, he was one of the most influential men in the West, a man of wealth, of stature, of prominence.

What more could the future hold for him?

Driving of the last spike at Promontory, Utah, on May 10, 1869, when the Central Pacific (now Southern Pacific) and Union Pacific were joined to form the first transcontinental railroad.

One of the first dining cars to be put in service on the Central Pacific Railroad.

7

TWO MARK HOPKINS' EMERGE

During the seven years of intense activity to complete the continental railroad, what had been happening to the two gentlemen known as Mark Hopkins? Both men had passed the half-century mark in ther lives. During this period both men had prospered, one much more than the other, of course, but each had a secure future. As the one continued the pattern of his earlier life, the other gradually dropped all traces of his former existence, in one way retreating from the community life, in another, advancing to lead and control not only his immediate community but his adopted state. The Mark Hopkins of North Carolina was no longer a simple country farmer, nor an experienced miner, nor partner in a comparatively restricted wholesale business. He was, instead, fast becoming one of the new millionaires of the West. He was a director of a complicated, far-reaching, and highly influential corporation. He had stepped out of the class of the Mark Hopkins of New York and other local merchants and businessmen to become a national figure of power. Yet in his personal life he had retreated more and more from the public eye, whereas the Mark Hopkins of New York was living the kind of family life and social existence expected of a treasurer of a railroad company.

After the first conference with Theodore Judah and other Sacramento merchants in the upstairs conference room of 54 K Street in 1860, Mark Hopkins of North Carolina found himself swept up into one of the most significant business transactions ever initiated in the United States. Whatever pursuits had previously occupied his limited leisure time were now abandoned in favor of the pressing tasks in the building of the Central Pacific Railroad. With the other members of what was to become the Big Four of California, he worked steadily, secretly, brilliantly, and successfully. All his energies, his talents, and his earnings went into the successful operation of one of the biggest firms in America. His devotion to his work was phenomenal. His capacity for remembering minute details of complex agreements and business transactions was readily admitted.

Though the other three may have been as deeply interested in working toward a successful and profitable corporation, they seemed to have had the time for a private and social life. The other three in the Big Four were younger than Hopkins; not so many of their youthful years had gone into the kind of hard work and plugging endurance that had characterized his life. The other three had married and had established families and homes that were to become centers for California social life. Presumably they enjoyed the comforts and pleasures of men of growing wealth.

But Mark Hopkins' private life was simple and relatively inconspicuous, being notable only because it was so restricted. Hopkins had no wife, no unit around which to build a private existence. His only relative in California was Moses, hardly a companion for the serious, hard-working Mark.

Moses was also a burden to Mark, always a source of anxiety, always the reason for Mark's reluctance to appear in the public eye, to discuss the background of his family life. Then it must be remembered that while the other three railroad magnates were still in the prime of life, Hopkins had already passed the fifty-year mark by the time the giant corporation was in its initial stage of growth. More than half his life expectancy was over, whereas the other three had still many years of life to anticipate.

Added to these reasons for a restricted private existence was the fact of Hopkins' bachelorhood. For good and sufficient reasons he had been unable to return to North Carolina and pick up the threads of his early romance. Mark Hopkins always desired and intended to marry his boyhood sweetheart, Elizabeth Jordan. Yet a fiancé thousands of miles away for a long, dreary period cannot expect to hold the affection and loyalty of a young woman. Thinking always of Elizabeth, waiting for the right time to marry her, Mark finally sent for her. But he was too late. There came to him the shocking, painful news that Elizabeth Jordan had been won by another, was already married, and could never become his wife. The announcement was a death blow to the emotional life of Mark Hopkins, a blow from which he never really recovered. People used to ask him why he did not marry and have a family. Mark always replied in the same, sad voice: "I have already given my heart to one woman, and I can never give it to another." Without any doubt, the cruel disappointment at the collapse of his romance caused Mark Hopkins to turn more and more to the affairs of business and to treat these affairs with the kind of affection and loving solicitude generally reserved for a wife and children.

In the meantime, the Mark Hopkins of New York had continued to operate his grocery business and to buy and sell real estate. His younger brother, Ezra Augustus, had become a successful farmer in Solano County. As a matter of fact, on January 2, 1863, he had appeared in the United States Land Office at Stockton, California, and there completed his application for the final deed to his homestead. He had fulfilled the requirements of the 1841 and the 1853 Congressional Acts governing homestead lands. Along with his preemption affidavit it was necessary for him to have a notarized statement from another person, preferably a relative, swearing to his right to the land. Since Ezra's brother Mark was unable to go to the Land Office with him, he asked his close neighbor and old friend Moses Hopkins to testify on his behalf. Moses agreed and on January 2, 1863, filled out the following affidavit before the Register of San Joaquin County:

In the matter of the claim of Ezra Hopkins of Solano Count to the Northeast quarter of Section 33, Township 4 North range one East, Mount Diablo Base and Meridan.

I, Moses Hopkins, being duly sworn touching the subject of inquiry, depose and say: I am of lawful age, with occupation being that of a farmer, am personally acquainted with Ezra Augustus Hopkins, Claimant of the above, *I have known him about ten years, or since 1852.* I know him to be a single man and a citizen of the United States, over twenty-one years of age. I have heard and read the above description of the land sought to be entered by the claimant, Ezra A. Hopkins, and know the premises. I know the claimant made a settlement on said land in person about July 1854, and has inhabited and improved the same and has erected a dwelling upon said premises. I know that he has since lived upon said land and made it his home and still continues to do so; that the said land is occupied solely for agriculture and not for trade; it is not within one mile of a military post. I have been over the land, and have held conversation in relation to it, and I do not know from my own personal knowledge or from heresay that there are any Silines, or Mines of any description on it, and I verily believe that there are none; that the claimant did not leave his residue on his own land or residue on the public land; I believe the claimant to be a bonafide preemptioner.

Sworn to and subscribed before me upon this 2nd day of January, 1863.

This document was signed by Moses Hopkins and the County Register, S. T. Myer. In addition, it was witnessed by J. M. Uphamm. The entire record is in the Land Office Department of the National Archives in Washington, D. C.

Though of small importance in itself, this document when related to the Mark Hopkins Controversy takes on great significance. First of all, the Moses Hopkins who wrote out the writ for the stay of judgment from the North Carolina Court in 1845 later testified as a preemption witness in 1863. Next, it definitely established that Ezra Augustus Hopkins was no blood relative of Moses Hopkins; rather, by his own statement, he was a friend known to him "about ten years, or since 1852." Yet seventeen years later, when Moses had no doubt forgotten all about his notorized declaration, he permitted the body of Ezra Augustus to be buried as a brother in the same tomb with his legitimate brother Mark; and later still, he authorized that his own body be placed in the same so-called family tomb. Thus in 1892 two men with the same last name were buried side by side as blood brothers, although thirty years before one had stated in a federal document that he had known the other for only ten years. History has a strange way of making itself known. A dusty little scrap of Land Office paper has proved that Ezra Augustus Hopkins and Moses Hopkins were in no way related to each other, having met in 1852 at the grocery store of Ezra's brother.

Two and a half years after Ezra Hopkins had secured title to his Solano County farm, he was stricken down by a sudden illness while visiting his brother in Sacramento. In a few days he was dead and his brother Mark decided to bury his body in the City Cemetery of Sacramento. In fact Mark, according to Deed Book 10 of Sacramento, purchased at the time a family burial lot in burial plot #0 in the City Cemetery, no doubt thinking that he and his wife would also be laid to rest beside his brother. The purchase was made on January 12, 1866. The Sacramento *Bee* of August 14, 1865, carries the following obituary: "In the City of Sacramento, August 14, E. A. Hopkins, a native of New York, age 43 years, 10 months, 23 days. Funeral at 4:00 o'clock tomorrow afternoon from the residence of his brother, Mark Hopkins, M St. between 3rd and 4th St. Friends of the family are respectfully invited to attend."

From the death of Ezra Augustus it is possible to learn a number of significant clues to the controversy. The residence of "Little" Mark Hopkins during the 1860's is given as M Street by the Sacramento *Bee*. Yet the City Directory for the same period lists 151 N Street as the address of

Mark Hopkins of the Huntington & Hopkins firm. These two addresses certify once more to the existence of two individuals named Mark Hopkins.

There were other individuals who were maturing and succeeding during the years 1860 to 1870. One of these was Edward H. Miller, Jr., friend and business associate of the grocery merchant, Mark Hopkins. By January of 1856 he had been able to buy out his partner, to change the name of his grocery store at 50 K Street to that of Miller & Company, and to become a close friend and business associate of the two men who operated Huntington & Hopkins. Naturally, when these two men became connected with the building of the Central Pacific Railroad, they had occasion to discuss matters with Miller. As the railroad line was rushed toward its eastern goal, the operations of the company expanded. The need for an increased administrative force became evident and E. H. Miller was among the first to be asked to join the company as a trusted employee. He was designated secretary of the company by the board of directors and, having sold out his store, Miller turned his attention to railroads, remaining the secretary for the board of directors for the rest of his life.

At this time other individuals joined the growing corporation. E. B. Crocker, brother of Charles Crocker, was appointed attorney for the company, and B. B. Redding was named land agent. Most interesting of all, the grocery merchant Mark Hopkins was employed as a treasurer for the corporation. Though these various business men held important positions in the Central Pacific and later the Southern Pacific Railroad, it must be remembered that their positions were those of employees, never those of owners and directors. From time to time the directors held such titular positions as president, secretary, treasurer, etc., even as in our own times the chairman of the board of directors of a large corporation may also for a time serve as president of the company, but just as easily may, with the other members of the board, designate a worthy and long-time employee as the president. Four men controlled the affairs and destiny of the railroads of the West. These four men—Stanford, Huntington, Hopkins, and Crocker—were the holders of the major portion of the stock of the corporation and it was they who as members of the board of directors established the policies. Their hired employees—such as E. B. Crocker, Miller, Redding, and the Mark Hopkins of New York—as trusted and able administrative officials, carried out the directives of the board. Though Hopkins of New York was a treasurer of the Central Pacific Railroad, he was not the owner of controlling shares of stock; he was not a millionaire railroad magnate.

It was coincidence that two men of the same name should be associated in the same company, handling similar aspects of the company's work. However, they were not the only Hopkins' in the corporation. Several Hopkins' worked in the treasury department of the railroad. Not only did the New York Mark Hopkins officiate in the treasury department, but his four nephews, one of whom was named after him, were also employees in the same department. "Young" Mark worked on the accounts for a good many years before he retired to his home town of St. Clair. A younger brother, Edward W. Hopkins, became his uncle's chief assistant and another, Samuel A. Hopkins, was an officer in the Contract and Finance Company. Later he became private secretary to the "Big" Mark Hopkins. Two other Brothers, William and Orin Hopkins, were treasurers in the branch offices of the Central Pacific Railroad, one in San Francisco and the other in Sheridan. Nepotism was an accepted business procedure back in the nineteenth century and such an inbred organization as the Central Pacific used the abilities of all relatives who qualified. Since Mark Hopkins of New York was an old and trusted friend of the members of the board of directors, it was natural that his nephews should be readily employed by the company. One more point should be made: the name "Mark Hopkins" was signed by many a company official working in the treasury department, even as the signature of the treasurer or vice-president of, let us say, R. H. Macy & Company, Inc. may be signed by an employee of the treasury department or the department of the general manager.

Other events were taking place in Mark Hopkins' life besides those connected with the railroad. Thirteen years after he and his brother had journeyed out into Solano County, their purchase of 160 acres was completed legally. Though Mark had filed the preemption claim, it was Moses who had actually farmed it, erected a good-sized house on the property, built a barn, set out and orchard, cultivated the most fertile ten acres, and cleared space for a chicken yard. A few head of cattle grazed on several fenced meadows. Wanting Moses to be rewarded for his perseverance, Mark on June 6, 1867, signed a document abandoning his claim to the south-east quarter of Section 33. A month later, Moses appeared at the same office, the United States Land Office in San Francisco, and with two witnesses to testify to his residence on the claim, was granted deed to the property. He paid 200 dollars for the 160 acres which he had lived on and improved. The complete record of these transactions and testimonials are preserved as No. 1373 of the San Francisco Land Office Records, now stored in the National Archives. These documents contain the signature of Moses Hopkins and the signature of Mark Hopkins, his brother.

Thereafter Moses expanded his agricultural activities, buying another large piece of grazing land in Nicolaus township, Sutter County, some miles north-east of his original homestead. The United States Census of 1870 lists Moses Hopkins of Sutter County as a farmer and notes that he was a native of Missouri. This latter piece of information was the closest Moses ever came to admitting his Southern origins. The value of his real estate in this census was given as 20,000 dollars and that of his personal estate as 10,000 dollars. These figures are in such marked contrast to the one and two thousand dollar estates listed by his neighbors that one can only assume that Mark Hopkins was contributing generously to the land speculations and personal income of his brother.

Another source of information on the lives and fortunes of the various individuals involved in this controversy are the city directories of Sacramento and San Francisco for the years 1950, 1860, and 1870. Though the purpose of these directories was to give the names, business and residential addresses, occupations, and birth places of the male citizens of the city, their great value in fixing such data must be weighed against the numerous possibilities for error and confusion. The checkers who were hired by the publishers of the directories were, after all, untrained individuals, not experienced in accurate canvassing. Secondly, many individuals were reluctant to reveal anything of their past, particularly their former residences. California law protected them from having to state their former homes; consequently many former criminals, such as Moses, were protected from extradition to another state.

In spite of these drawbacks in using the city directories as a final source, it is necessary to correlate the information in them with other more reliable sources. Tracing the entries for Mark Hopkins through the years, one is at first bewildered and then amused to note that he is credited with being a native of New York, of Massachusetts, and of Kentucky, and that for many years no place of birth is given. In the same way, Huntington is said to have been a native of both Connecticut and New York, and Charles Crocker's birth state is listed as Indiana and New York.

Very likely the compilers of the directories did not differentiate between the two Mark Hopkins', and sometimes the three Mark Hopkins'. At times Mark Hopkins is listed as the treasurer of the Central Pacific Railroad, sometimes as belonging to the firm of Huntington & Hopkins, sometimes as both. In some instances his residence address is given, in others his business number. Sometimes he is listed as a married man and others as a bachelor. Here then is one of the first instances in which the two men are confused, and also the first instance, whether accidental or intentional, of the blending of the two men's lives and positions, as well as marital status. To add further to the confusion, no dircetory now in existence (the volumes are not complete for every year) lists two Mark Hopkins' in either Sacramento or San Francisco.

The fact that the missing volumes of the city directories are the same in every library consulted may be accidental or it may be part of a deliberate effort to withdraw significant documents from public circulation. The misinformation in the 1870 United States Census for the city of Sacramento, however, cannot be accepted as an accident. Here, is the kind of source material which historians have come to respect and to use as the basis for interpretations, we find a shocking attempt to distort the lives and fortunes of two men. In an effort to change the New York Mark Hopkins into the figure of the railroad magnate, someone has altered the entry for the Mark Hopkins household. The entry as it now stands states that Mark Hopkins was a treasurer of a railroad company, that he came from New York, as did his wife Mary F. Hopkins, who kept house, that a nine-year-old boy named Timothy Nolan lived with them, and that they had a Chinese domestic servant, Ah Sing. From other sources, we know that this entry is correct, since by 1870 Mark Hopkins of New York had given up his grocery business, as had his former partner, E. H. Miller, and both of them were working for the Central Pacific Railroad.

The entry then goes on to give the value of Mark Hopkins' real estate as 9150 dollars and the value of his personal estate as 8,655,180 dollars. The last figure is arresting, since multimillionaires are rare enough today and in 1870 were even rarer. However, it is not the staggering sum that is of paramount interest in the case; what is significant is that the figures have obviously been changed. The original personal property figure has been erased. Close examination shows it to have been a number of only four, not seven digits. Handwriting experts have testified that the eight-million-dollar figure is written in a different hand and in a different ink from the rest of the census page and, most important of all, that this figure was added to the Mark Hopkins entry quite a few years after the original entries.

The document expert, Charles A. Appel of Washington, D.C., examined the original census report for 1870 and has made the following analysis of the Mark Hopkins listing given there:

As requested, the original entry on line 19, page 4, schedule 1, Census of 4th Ward, Sacramento, California, 1870, opposite the name Mark Hopkins, was examined for erasure and alteration of the figures showing value of Real Estate and Value of Personal Estate. This document is in the Archives of the U. S.

It is concluded that the plainly apparent erasures of the amount of Real Estate and Personal Estate of Mark Hopkins were made with an abrasive instrument which removed part of the paper surfaces.

Under the present amount for Personal Estate, "8,655,150" the erasure appears ½ line below without any figures being written over the erasure. Examined under the microscope, the original lines of ink were seen to have been "4250."

Under the present amount for Real Estate "9150" which is written over the erased figures, examination by microscope shows the "5" and "0" under the present "50" were erased and rewritten. Under the "91" (hundred), lines were found conforming with "44." This is clear as to the second "4" and less clear as to the "9" written over "4" since the erased lines coincide nearly with the erased and rewritten ones so that the "9" upper part conceals part of the upper part of "4." It is the best judgment of the examiner that the erased figure was "4450."

At the bottom of the columns for the page total figures are shown and these were examined for erasures but none were found. The total for Real Estate is added incorrectly to "44050" when it should be "47050." The total for Personal Estate includes the changed amount for Mark Hopkins and is added correctly to "8,682,250." It is not clear that the columns were habitually totalled. The forms of the figures are of a style design resembling those of use in the 19th century more than now but not similar to those in the individual entries down the page and use of this design does not prove that the entries of totals were made contemporaneous with compilation of the document originally. The ink has brown tones much blacker than the rest of the entries which have turned completely brown in the manner typical of iron ink written in the times more than 10 years ago (not much change occuring thereafter). Similarly the ink of the changes opposite Mark Hopkins name is still black compared with the brown color of the unchanged entries and obviously was not written at the same date. From the color alone no accurate estimate of the actual age of the changed entries may be made.

By chemical analysis test in which reagents are applied directly to the paper bearing the altered ink it is possible to ascertain whether there are now present in the ink chlorides and sulphates, which in the course of time spread out away from the ink lines into the paper fibers until the disappear.

The same type of tests may be made by applying blank sheets of paper over the changed entries, pressed down tightly to the surface and left for an interval. Migration of chlorides into these test papers in the same way chlorides migrate away from the ink lines to areas of the document itself, would then be tested for which reagents applied to the test papers and not to the document which would remain untouched with any substance which might change it. Development on the test papers of the chlorides would then prove that the changes were made within the past two years if average conditions of storage were present after being written. Development of sulphates would indicate a longer time but would show that the changes could not have been made at the time of the original entries.

In the absence of such tests the only evidence of when the changes were made is the color of the ink which is less than that normally chaged from black to brown in 7 to 10 years.

In connection with the figure "8,655,150" substituted for "4250" in the personal estate space for Mark Hopkins, attention is invited to the possibility that this figure was arrived at on the spur of the moment while erasing the original figures. If no real figures were at hand from some source which might be used and it was simply desired to substitute some large figure more appropriate to Mark Hopkins than $4250, some sum would have to be guessed. It would only be natural, therefore, to unconsciously use figures at hand which were being changed. If, starting at the left of the figures in the spaces, digits were added independently of each other, the first two figures "86" would be derived from addition of "44" and "42" in the sums "4450" and "4250." The next digits proceedings toward the right, in the enlarged sum of Personal Estate are "55" and the next digits both originally and now in Real Estate "5" and erased Personal Estate "5" could therefore account for the "55" digits following the "86 (55)." The remaining three digits it will be noted agree with the digits "150" ending the number "9150" to which the Real Estate was changed and were therefore in the mind of the person making the change. This speculation is of course pure theory based on the digits selected, and is offered only as one possible explanation of the amount in the event it does not agree with any reported or estimated amount of the actual Personal Estate of the Mark Hopkins of the Railroad ownership at that time.

During the examination of the Census document in Archives it was handled with great care, being untouched in the area under examination.

Sincerely yours,
Charles A. Appel, Jr.

As a matter of fact, when the 1870 census report was first consulted by the North Carolina heirs of Mark Hopkins in the 1930's, it recorded the value of Hopkins' personal estate in the thousands. A photostat was made but was lost some years later. When the heirs returned to the record to obtain another copy, they found that one item had been altered, but it was the most telling one since it helped to establish the Mark Hopkins of New York as the millionaire railroad owner. Huntington, Crocker, and Stanford were all listed as millionaires in the census and to be consistent, Hopkins had to be listed similarly. The Mark Hopkins of North Carolina had for some reason not been included in the 1870 census; thus it was simple for forgers to make it appear that the New York personage was the railroad associate.

Crediting Mark Hopkins of New York with a personal estate comparable to that of Huntington, Stanford, and Crocker, however, did not quite take care of it. The hand that altered the record had forgotten to include the fact that the railroad financier was also a merchant. As a partner in the wealthy firm of Huntington & Hopkins in 1870, the millionaire should also have been listed as a merchant as well as a railroad associate. He would also have been listed as director of the Central Pacific, not merely as "treasurer of a railroad company."

To substantiate the existence of two Mark Hopkins', there are several personal testimonies which distinguish clearly between the two individuals of Sacramento and later of San Francisco. Two are in the form of affidavits sworn out in the presence of notary publics, and the third is an account given to one of the North Carolina heirs in the presence of four witnesses. They help to confirm the thesis of this volume: that the railroad capitalist was from North Carolina, that he was not married to Mary Frances Sherwood, and that he was the victim of confusion with another and a lesser person.

Robert Young Reed of North Carolina has made the following sworn statement:

> . . . I am reasonably well acquainted in the Russell Mine section of Montgomery County, Eldorado Township, State of North Carolina, having worked in said mine some seven months, following the Civil War . . . During said seven months employment I learned to know the location and home place of Edward Hopkins (commonly known as "Neddie Hopkins"). . . . I also learned to know John and Martin Hopkins, sons of the said Edward Hopkins, residents of the same community. . . . Some time later in my travels as an itinerant missionary I went to California and visited the mining sections of that state. While at one of these mines I met and formed the acquaintance of Mark Hopkins, who stated to me that he was a son of the aforesaid Edward Hopkins and was reared at the aforesaid Hop-

kins home; also that my old acquaintances, the aforesaid John and Martin Hopkins were his (Mark Hopkins') brothers. In the trend of conversation he made inquiry of a number of old friends and relatives of said Russell Mine Section. Mark Hopkins stated to me that he had four sisters in North Carolina near the said Russell Mine; also that the aforesaid Barnie Hopkins was a relative. He told me that his brother Moses was living there in California with him and that he (Moses) would be glad to see me. A day or such a matter later I met said Moses Hopkins at a station. He approached me and stated that his brother Mark Hopkins had told him of meeting me a few days previous . . . I Robert Young Reed do herein swear that I recognize the photographs of Mark and Moses Hopkins respectively upon their presentation to me, and declare that they are the photographs of the men, Mark and Moses Hopkins, whom I met in California; the same Mark and Moses Hopkins herein before mentioned. I further state that the said Mark and Moses Hopkins were men much older than at the time I met them in California.

From Sacramento came another sworn statement from two elderly ladies who were breaking up their home and selling their family furniture. Some of the Hopkins heirs, learning that a few of the pieces had been a gift of Mark Hopkins, were anxious to buy these items, since no genuine family heirlooms remained for the North Carolina family. The two ladies were glad to tell what little they knew of Mark Hopkins and incorporated their information into the notarized bill of sale:

. . . we hereby, assign and transfer to Estelle Latta one parlor suite of furniture consisting of eight pieces of walnut upholstered with black horsehair, viz. one settee, two arm chairs, four stool chairs and one hassock, presented to our father Henry Treichler for his new home at No. 1926 H. Street, Sacramento by Mark Hopkins, a bachelor and a member of the "Big Four," Huntington, Hopkins, Stanford, and Crocker, in 1875. Mark Hopkins was an intimate friend of our father and was a bachelor with a brother, Moses Hopkins, who resided on a large stock ranch at East Nichols, Sutter County, California.

Some years ago, a Mrs. Wise of Sacramento was able to tell investigating attorneys much of interest about the two Hopkins families. She had grown up in Sacramento during the 1860's and personally remembered and had been acquainted with both Marks and with their brothers. She very kindly related what she remembered about the men and her relationship with them.

My father and mother used to run a boarding house at Folsom, California. In those days it was quite a big place not far from the mining areas around Placerville and Marysville. The Sacramento Valley railroad ran through the town and Folsom was one of the principal stations for freight as well as passengers going to the mines. It was here that I first met the Northern family of Hopkins when I was a young girl. I also met Edward H. Miller, William Hopkins, "Young" Mark Hopkins, and Mrs. Mary Frances Hopkins there. They used to come up to Folsom on some kind of railroad business and would always stay at my parents' boarding house. My mother was always rather frantic when they showed up because Mrs. Hopkins was such a fussy woman. I remember her setting up a special table for their family and going to a lot of extra trouble to make things nice for them, especially Mrs. Hopkins. William and "Young" Mark were introduced as nephews of Mr. Hopkins and they were supposed to be learning accounting for the railroad company. Once when they all came, there was another man with them, a brother of Mark Hopkins who lived on a farm somewhere outside of Sacramento.

<u>BILL OF SALE</u>

Sacramento, California.

For and in consideration of the sum of Seven Hundred
and Fifty Dollars ($750.00) to us in hand paid by A. S.
BLOUNT for ESTELLE LATTA, we hereby sell, assign and
transfer to ESTELLE LATTA one parlor suite of furniture
consisting of Eight pieces of walnut upholstered with
black horsehair, viz. one settee, two arm chairs, four stool
chairs and one hassock, presented to our father HENRY TREICHLER
for his new home at No. 1926 H Street, Sacramento, by Mark
Hopkins a batchlor and a member of the "Big Four", Huntington,
Hopkins, Stanford and Crocker, in 1875. Mark Hopkins was an
intimate friend of our father and a batchlor with a brother
Mose Hopkins who resided on a large stock ranch at East
Nichols, Sutter County, California.

Dated, Sacramento, California, December 27th, 1950.

Miss Hattie Treichler
Mrs. P. E. Jones

STATE OF CALIFORNIA. } ss.
County of Sacramento
On this....7th....day of....September....in the year one thousand nine hundred and....fifty one....
before me....D. G. Hunneley....a Notary Public in and for the County of Sacramento,
personally appeared....Hattie Treichler and Mrs P E Jones....

known to me to be the person..s.. whose name..s.. ..are.... subscribed to the within instrument, and
....duly acknowledged to me that ..the..y.. executed the same
IN WITNESS WHEREOF, I have hereunto set my hand and affixed my Official Seal the day and year in
this certificate first above written.

D. G. Hunneley
Notary Public in and for the County of Sacramento, State of California

My Commission expires....4/14 th ....1951....
(LM 8-45)

Notarized bill of sale describing
Mark Hopkins as a "batchlor."

Some time later my father and mother gave up their place in Folsom and we moved to Sacramento, to a house on L St. Mr. and Mrs. Hopkins were the first visitors we had in our new house. I vividly remember that because my parents were so surprised that Mrs. Hopkins should have made a social call on them. She always seemed such a cold woman, sort of superior to other people, and my mother couldn't understand why she suddenly became so friendly. But we saw quite a bit of the Hopkins' after that. They lived fairly close to us, on M St., No. 139, I think, and I recall that several nephews lived with them at various times, for we saw them too.

I was never closely associated personally with the Southern Hopkins family, but I did know there were two brothers, Mark and Moses. I first saw them at a church service with my father and mother. As I was but a girl at the time, I suppose the only reason they made an impression upon me was because the pastor introduced them to Father after the service and they all talked together for what seemed ages. I thought I would starve before we could get home to dinner. In later years I continued to see them occasionally at the same church but they did not attend regularly. Usually they attended only special services of various sorts, and even then they did not always come together.

I remember well that people in Sacramento used to refer to the Hopkins as "Big" Mark and "Little" Mark and that "Young" Mark was the nephew of "Little" Mark. "Big" Mark used to talk with a slight lisp and people used to kid him about his slow Southern speech. I suppose some people got them mixed up, but anyone that knew either of them at all knew that one was a Yankee and the other a Southerner who made a lot of money in the Pacific Railroad.

When it became evident to the Big Four that their first venture into a major corporation was going to be a success, they began to plan for more rail lines and greater control

of the traffic, not only from the East, but throughout the
Pacific Coast area. So in 1870, with the final spikes driven
at Ogden, the business associates were ready to launch new
transportation projects. One of the first things they did
was to take over the construction of a line to run from
Sacramento to San Jose via Stockton. In 1869 the Central
Pacific had acquired the Sacramento Valley Railroad with
its extension to Placerville, and shortly after that they got
control of the California Central Railroad that ran from
Folsom to Marysville. If the Big Four were to control the
traffic of California and the West they would have to control
the line between Sacramento and San Francisco and to control the traffic in the San Joaquin Valley. To achieve these
objectives it was first necessary to secure a terminal on the
eastern side of San Francisco Bay. Since 1867, Stanford
had been negotiating with Horace W. Carpentier for property rights in and along the Oakland waterfront. To promote this project, the Central Pacific Railroad established
offices in San Francisco, and gradually the associates moved
their private homes to the Golden Gate city.

Stanford organized the Oakland Water Front Company,
to which Carpentier deeded the entire waterfront of Oakland. In turn the company deeded 500 acres of this choice
waterfront property to the Western Pacific Railroad and
granted an exclusive right-of-way to the entire area. It was
another example of the associates' use of subsidiary companies
to gain strength and power and profits for the founding
organization. Citizens of Oakland were in an uproar over
the "steal" by the Central Pacific of this strategic commercial
site. The Company tried to pacify the citizenry by deeding

a large portion of the land to the city, but bitterness and complaints continued for years. Nevertheless, the Central Pacific was overjoyed with its success in securing so much waterfront property. With it, they had a coastal terminal and control of a half-mile frontage for the ship channel. With it, their transportation lines could extend in all directions from San Francisco.

By 1873 permanent offices were erected for the Central Pacific and its subsidiaries at the north-east corner of Fourth and Townsend Streets in San Francisco. A year earlier, Huntington, Hopkins & Co. had established a branch store at the junction of Bush and Market Streets and were listed in the San Francisco City Directory as importers and jobbers and dealers in hardware and metals. Thus the scene was set for the gradual transfer of management from Sacramento to San Francisco.

Leland Stanford was the first to move. Collis P. Huntington maintained his residence in New York City where he continued to safeguard and promote the interests of the railroad among Eastern leaders. Charles Crocker, always the restless member of the quartet, lived first at the Occidental Hotel and later in the more spacious Palace Hotel. "Big" Mark Hopkins stayed on in Sacramento for a few more years, reluctant to leave the city he had grown to love and anxious to remain in control not only of the still existing hardware house in Sacramento but also to watch over railroad affairs there. In the latter part of 1874 "Little" Mark Hopkins went to San Francisco to take over the offices of the treasury department there. He rented a house at 1105 Taylor Street and there Mary Frances managed the household which by that time included Mark's nephews, Edward and Samuel, and a young boy, Timothy Nolan.

A word should be said here about this young boy. He was the son of New England pioneers. His father had died during the long overland journey to California in 1862 and after the survivors of the party reached Sacramento, his mother applied for work at Mark Hopkins' truck farm outside the city. The poor widow's infant son, Timothy, won the heart of her employer's wife and when Mrs. Nolan decided to remarry and move to a farm in Yolo County, she agreed to leave her youngest son with the Hopkins family to be brought up as their own son. Timothy later wrote: "I was reared in his famly from infancy and knew no other parents." When he was thirteen, Timothy moved to San Francisco with the Hopkins' and continued to receive his education there. After Mark Hopkins died, his wife Mary Frances legally adopted the boy and gave him the name of Timothy Hopkins. In the later law suits, he, together with his adopted mother, his adopted uncles, and Moses Hopkins, alleged that the Hopkins in New York, his adopted parent, was one of the Big Four millionaires. Although his testimony varied from time to time throughout the years, out-of-court settlements of several million dollars stopped him from ever confessing the truth about the deliberate confusion of the wealth and the names of the two Mark Hopkins'.

Meanwhile the growing giant corporation was reaching out its tentacles in every direction—north, south, east, and west. It had acquired the San Francisco and San Jose Railway, which had been built with the help of subsidiaries from

the two cities. To head off efforts of the Union Pacific to
get a western terminus at Portland, the Central Pacific constructed a road from San Francisco to Portland through the
Sacramento Valley, using the building genius and business
acumen of the Contract and Finance Company, builders of
the first line to Ogden. By 1887 this line, which succeeded
in strangling efforts of the Union Pacific to expand, was
completed at Ashland, Oregon. The company also turned
to construction of a railroad in the southern part of the state
that would permit them to control the agricultural development in that area, prevent the growth of rival lines into
the state, and give them in the future an independent line
to the East that would not be dependent on the Union
Pacific. A number of independent lines were acquired in the
San Joaquin Valley. At the same time the directors of the
Central Pacific began to eye the growth of a line known
as the Southern Pacific, which had received a charter in 1865
for construction of a road along the coast from San Jose to
San Diego. But in 1867 a change in the route was announced, giving the new line free monopoly of the southern
areas of the coast. Such an arrangement gave the Central
Pacific and the new Southern Pacific complete and absolute
rule of all railroad transportation in California. In 1871 it
was announced that the Contract and Finance Company, that
convenient construction organization controlled by the four
merchants of Sacramento, would build the Southern Pacific
Line from Gilroy to Fort Mojave. The world knew then
that the Big Four had taken over the Southern Pacific and
that thereafter one corporation would control the destiny
of transportation in the West. Subsequently the line man-

aged to move into Arizona, New Mexico, and Texas, eventually reaching New Orleans. The task of controlling a line from California to the East had been completed.

All of the various lines, short and long, had different names, but they were all under the control of the Central Pacific. To formalize the ownership, a corporation known as the Southern Pacific Company was chartered in the state of Kentucky in 1884, and through stock ownership and lease it has continued to control the combined properties of the Central and the Southern Pacific Railroad companies.

Meanwhile the enterprising four gentlemen from Sacramento and San Francisco proceeded to absorb, to buy, to steal, to build, and to manage nearly every other form of transportation then developing. Street car lines were acquired, steamship companies controlled, docks and warehouse stock purchased, etc., etc., etc. There was nothing in the form of traffic and transportation on the Pacific Coast which the four gentlemen did not know about and did not either buy out or acquire controlling shares in if that traffic or transportation threatened in the least to rival their undisputed lordship of the state of California. These men became the owners and rulers of the state for awhile. No business transaction was unethical to them; no private scruple was allowed to interfere with their plans for monopoly. Little wonder that such men were capable of the fraud involved in merging the characters and lives of two men into one personality—a personality that they could also control!

8

LAST YEARS

There is too much concurrence in the numerous newspaper reports of Mark Hopkins' character for it to be denied that the railroad magnate was a hard-working, highly responsible, and most frugal man. His romance with Elizabeth shattered, the rejected suitor turned more and more to the affairs of the railroad and its subsidiary companies as an outlet for his energies and interests. While the other railroad financiers and builders were beginning to enjoy the fruits of their profitable enterprises, Mark Hopkins continued to live in Sacramento and to behave as if he were not a millionaire at all, just a simple business man. The others moved to San Francisco and there in the Nob Hill District, which their palatial homes eventually made famous, began a social life of leisure and grandeur. In addition, they were becoming more absorbed in the larger society of the East. Huntington, particularly, resided in the East and became a conspicuous member of the socially elite there.

But Hopkins stayed on in Sacramento, resisting the efforts of his partners to get him to San Francisco. For a long time he also apparently did not indulge in the practice of taking profits out of the corporation, which the others had freely adopted. For instance, David Colton told Huntington in a letter that over a five-month period the members of the Big Four took the following sums from the company treasury for their personal accounts and expenses: Stanford, 276,000 dollars; Huntington, 57,000 dollars; Crocker, 31,000 dollars; and Mark Hopkins, 800 dollars.* No wonder Hopkins had the reputation for thrift and modesty that so many reporters commented upon! The Sacramento *Union* (March 30, 1878) added the other salient point in his personality: "He was an indefatigable worker; he was ever employed; to be busy was the habit of his life."

Commendable as such attention and industry were, they inevitably took their toll in reduced health and vigor. For years Hopkins refused to recognize that he was anything but strong and alert, with many years ahead of him. He did not take trips to Europe, nor did he allow himself any long vacations. Until he was sixty years of age, he treated his body as he treated his work—firmly, positively, and unemotionally. He continued to eat little—indeed his sparrow-like appetite was the wonder of acquaintances who themselves tucked away five and six course meals daily without apparent strain. He neither smoked nor drank and what little he ate was consumed from a sense of necessity rather than pleasure. Never a robust man, his lean, rather awkward figure was a familiar one in the streets of Sacramento.

But as Hopkins grew older, he became increasingly aware of his aching knee and ankle joints. Rheumatism was beginning to limit his activities and prevent him from being as efficient as his younger partners. Undoubtedly one of the reasons why he was so reluctant to move to San Francisco

---

* Letter from David Colton to Collis P. Huntington.

was that he knew the damp, foggy climate there would only aggravate his rheumatism and he wished to avoid such additional pain and strain on his system for as long as possible. By the middle of the 1870's Hopkins had moved to San Francisco and there arranged for the construction of a large mansion in the Nob Hill District. Meanwhile he had agreed to take summer vacations, though he stoutly refused to retire from active business affairs. "He was urged to retire; and for a season each year he did betake himself to a favorite retreat in the mountains, where he lived in a modest cabin and dwelt in the very heart of nature." *

This modest cabin in the mountains was much more interesting to Mark Hopkins than the grand mansion being built for him in San Francisco. The Nob Hill house was for show, a mansion to glorify the success of the railroad magnates and to add an expensive front to the rapidly developing city of San Francisco. As one writer put it: "It is known to many of his friends that he simply built the mansion for the hereafter—not for himself. He did not expect to enjoy it—in fact he much preferred the little log cabin in the Sierras." †

In the 1870's Hopkins and Stanford had financed a summer mountain resort in the Sierras near Soda Springs. Located at an altitude of 6784 feet, Soda Springs, long known as Hopkins' Spring, is situated in Summit Valley in the shadow of Donner Pass. Heavy snows, such as those that destroyed the famous Donner Party journeying through it, continued to blanket these wilderness mountains,

* Sacramento *Union*, March 30, 1878.
† Sacramento *Bee*, March 29, 1878.

but in summer Soda Springs is a lovely, cool spot, as Mark Hopkins well knew. Although much more rugged, much higher, and much less settled, the area reminded him of the hills of the Southern highlands where he had spent so many happy days as a boy fishing and hunting. He reserved a certain portion of the resort area for himself and built on it a one-room log cabin far from the main lodge halls and popular hiking and riding trails. The isolation, the simplicity of natural beauty, and the way of life in the mountain retreat made the one-room cabin an ideal spot for Mark Hopkins—a place where he could again feel active and energetic.

From a reporter for the Sacramento *Bee*, we get the following concise description of Hopkins at this time: "Just before the removal of the offices (to San Francisco) he began to feel rather less vigorous than usual and was advised to rest. But work was his hobby, and he continued with his enormous labors. It began to tell more and more upon his constitution and his mind, and some years ago he was told to stop all work. To divert his mind and rest his body he retired to Soda Springs in the Sierras and built for himself a beautiful log cabin, amused himself by making trails, clearing brush, catching fish, and lying under the pines. He scarcely read letter or newspaper and knew little of what was going on in the world. But returning to San Francisco, the association would bring him back to work again and next summer he would again have to recuperate." *

Though the railroad magnate's health was failing, he did outlive the Mark Hopkins of New York. Sometime in the

* March 29, 1878.

late months of 1876 or the early part of the 1877 the latter died. Unfortunately, no record has ever been found of his death, but the time has been established pretty accurately from the date that social notices regarding Mr. and Mrs. Mark Hopkins stopped appearing in the newspapers. How he died, where he died, and on what day remain mysteries. All clues concerning his last years have disappeared. For those who were perhaps even then scheming to claim the estate of Hopkins, the railroad magnate, it was a most opportune death.

Piecing together the reminiscences and inferences of various personal reports by persons who knew of the existence of the two Mark Hopkins', we learn some interesting details. After her husband's death, Mary Frances left San Francisco and went to visit her old friend Moses Hopkins who was still living on his Sutter County ranch. The two had met years before at Ezra Hopkins' farm and had carried on a secret flirtation. Moses had considerable reputation for amorous adventures and the wife of his old friend seems to have been among his conquests. As the story goes, Mary Frances lived for some months with Moses until he deserted her in favor of a local hairdresser who won his affections by claiming she could produce hair on his bald head. Mary Frances was incensed but helpless. She had no home of her own any longer—no place where she and her adopted son Timothy could go to live. Moses suggested that she appeal to his brother Mark. He never turned away an old friend, Moses insisted, and would probably welcome the wife of an old business associate. He pointed out that Mark was ill a good part of the time and would doubtless be glad to have

The only U.S. Census record in which Moses Hopkins' name appears (Entry #18). Note that he gave his birthplace as Missouri, presumably to conceal his identity as a fugitive from North Carolina justice.

1870 U. S. Census record, containing entries for Mark Hopkins of New York, his wife Mary F. Hopkins, and Timmy Nolan, who was later adopted and became Timothy Hopkins (Entries #19, 20, 21). Note the altered figures under "Value of Real Estate Owned." This alteration was made sometime in the 1940's.

someone to care for his quarters, cook his meals, and look after his health. At the time, Mark was engaged with the construction of his mansion on Nob Hill and a woman's touch would be useful to the execution of plans. Mark accepted Mrs. Hopkins as his housekeeper. In this favorable position, she was later able to make her claim to wifehood to the Mark Hopkins of North Carolina more plausible. Yet her own adopted son Timothy told witnesses that his adopted mother had never lived in the same house with the railroad magnate, but that she had worked there in the daytime, returning to her own home at night. He said: "She was never considered the wife of the railroad magnate—that she was only a housekeper who drew a weekly salary of five dollars."

By the summer of 1877 Mark Hopkins realized that he had only a few years to live. Before he died he had a desire to see once more the place of his birth and to visit with his brothers and sisters who had remained in North Carolina. Although none of the newspapers of the day mention the fact, witnesses have testified in court that Mark Hopkins did visit Randolph County during the year 1877. It is not odd that the papers carried no such notice. Hopkins was by nature an extremely modest person who rarely revealed any information or personal facts. He was hardly the man to want to publicize his return home. His normal inclination would have been to slip away quietly and travel across the country without any fuss.

Although some of the witnesses who testified that Mark Hopkins had been in Randolph County in 1877 were children or were in their teens at the time of his visit, the fact that they could recall his presence more than fifty years later strengthens the contention that his trip made a long-lasting impression upon the neighborhood. It is interesting to note that the wealthy man from California remained loyal to his friends and relatives of North Carolina and showed himself to be "a man of retiring habits but genial disposition, and though not seeking friendships, never rejecting worthy ones." * Besides describing certain aspects of Mark Hopkins' character and affirming his interest in North Carolina kin, the testimony on his visit verifies the fact that the Mark Hopkins of North Carolina was the railroad capitalist.

Mr. M. C. Elam, the old miner who described in an earlier chapter the Hopkins' visit to Gold Hill in 1877, added: "He told Joe [Joseph Hopkins, Mark Hopkins' brother] that if he ever heard of his death, he and Moses both wanted to be brought home and buried by their mother and father in the old cemetery by the persimmon tree . . . He said he and his brother Joe went down to the old round swimming hole where he used to fish with pin hooks and go in bathing. He said there was a bend in the creek where they got minnows; they all called it the old swimming hole . . . He [Mark Hopkins] was a sort of full-faced man with a short beard on his face."

Mrs. Nora Yates, a grand-niece of Mark Hopkins, recalled his visit to her home and to her grandmother, Rebecca Hopkins: " I saw Mark once, when I was a little kid; he came back here and my grandmother came with him to our house. He came in his short sleeves to our house . . . She [Rebecca Hopkins] called him brother."

* Sacramento *Union*, March 30, 1878.

Mr. W. L. Cranford remembered Mark Hopkins' visit to his brother Martin in this way: "I worked a lot at Uncle Martin's in my boyhood. He was a brother of Mark. I don't remember how old I was, twelve of thirteen. I was working on the farm for Uncle Martin and a man came there and it proved to be Mark Hopkins; came there on a visit. He and Uncle Martin went around visiting their brothers and sisters. He had a grandson, John, who worked with me. He said that his grandpa's brother was from the West." He further recollects conversations about Mark Hopkins in the family circle: "I have heard about it lots of times. They said that Mark was in there and they were living alone, brother and sister, didn't have a wife or husband; they were leaving and I heard them say that Mark wanted them to go home with him to California. They spoke several times about the Pacific Railroad, that he had an interest, I don't know that I could say how much interest, in the Pacific Railroad."

Mr. John H. Milton, who lived in Albemarle, Stanly County, in 1877, was much impressed by the tall stranger from California who visited his town: "I saw him with that beautiful beard, sort of like Lee Freeman has now. I asked my father who that good-looking bearded man was over there at the store, at Mr. Freeman's. Their father had a store in Albemarle. He said, 'Son, that is Mark Hopkins from California; he is considered a very rich man.' About that time Sheriff Marshall came up and said to my father, 'Have you been over to shake hands with Mark yet? I have just come from over there.' He said, 'No, but I am going, we were all raised together.' "

The examining attorney asked Mr. Milton about Mark Hopkins' appearance and instructed him to look at the picture reproduced in Daggett's *Chapters on the History of the Southern Pacific* (the same picture that appears facing title page of this book.) Mr. Milton scrutinized the portrait and said, "That is a good picture of him. His hair was nice and slick and he was dressed up real nice. He was a good-looking fellow."

To emphasize this point the attorney asked him, "Is that picture the same man that you saw?" Mr. Milton replied, "Yes, sir."

Mr. Milton had worked as a superintendent in a soldiers' home for nearly five years in the 1870's and had had previous knowledge of Mark Hopkins from a nephew who was one of his patients. He relates: "And he had a nephew, his brother's son; I read letters to him that Mark wrote to him. That was in 1875 and 1876. I did that at the soldiers' home. [These letters] were begging Bennie Hopkins to come out there—they had plenty of everything—for him to come out there and live . . . I think some of them were written from Sacramento, California. He told me if I'd cure him he would go out there and try to look up what interest he could find there; he knew there was a great interest there for the Hopkins family, and he wanted to go. I said, 'You should have gone when they wrote you those letters; then you would have been boss.' "

Another old family friend, Mr. E. L. Hardister, who spent his school days in the same Randolph County settlement with the nephews and nieces of Hopkins, recalls: "I saw him in 1877 when he came here, at my brother-in-law's,

Walker's. I stayed with him at my brother-in-law's all night and would have gone home with him if it hadn't been for my brother who was going to attend lectures in Baltimore. Hopkins offered me a hundred dollars a month if I'd go back and work with him." He then told the examiner that Mark Hopkins "had a heap of stock in different railroads and some other business, some kind of hardware."

E. L. Chandler, a grand-niece of Mark Hopkins, said: "He and Miles Hopkins came to Edy Hopkins on horseback and hitched their horses on the back side of the house to a peach tree and they gnawed the bark off . . . Said he went to California, he and Moses."

Mrs. Sula Koppelmeyer, another grand-niece, told of the time her father visited a relative in middle Tennessee and saw Mark Hopkins there: "Pa told him he was going to leave Tennessee; he had been there teaching school about eight years. Mark told him to come to California. Pa was well pleased with the idea; he would have gone, and he said to ma, 'I am going to California; Mark and Moses want me to move to California; what about going there?' She said, 'I don't want to go where it never rains, and I'm not going'; and they didn't go."

The last witness who remembered Mark Hopkins' visit to North Carolina in 1877 and told about it in the North Carolina Supreme Court was Mr. Norman Lee Freeman. A grand-nephew of Mark and Moses Hopkins, he testified that Mark Hopkins' home at the time of the visit was in San Francisco, California. "He and my grandfather, Eli Russell, went to my father's store on horseback. I recollect Grandfather rode a kind of a sorrel horse, called Mat, and

Uncle Mark was on a flea-bitten one named Dargin, but Grandpa called him 'Dergin.' Uncle Mark was anxious for his nephew Jones to go back with him to California. Jones had just graduated from college and he wanted him to assist him in his office in San Francisco."

Cheered and happy at seeing his old friends and neighbors, at visiting again the scenes of his childhood, Mark Hopkins returned to his work in San Francisco. He had been unable to persuade any of his relatives to join him in the West. This doubtless disappointed him. He most certainly would have enjoyed helping them and he would have found pleasure in their companionship. Since no will has been found belonging to the railroad magnate, we have, of course, no indication of how he meant to distribute his estate. Yet the fact that he made a visit during his last years to North Carolina, that he visited at length with his relatives, that he wanted to be buried in North Carolina—these indicate a strong loyalty to his family. Such a man, with free will and sound mind, would most likely have wished his estate to be divided among his legal heirs.

On his return to California, Hopkins was presented with many troubling problems. There was the house that was gradually taking shape on California and Mason Streets. There were the vast debts that were calling for immediate settlement on the part of the Central Pacific Railroad. Congressional pressures were being brought to bear on the management of the company. Huntington was frantic for the future financial security of the railroad; Colton was demanding economy in the disbursement of earnings; bitterness, disagreements, struggles for dominance were beginning to enter into what had formerly been a most harmonious union of talents.

As winter approached with its rain and fog, Mark's rheumatism returned with greater force. Though he suffered from the pain in his knees and ankles, he continued to apply himself to these multiple problems. He refused to become an invalid. With the aid of two canes he was able to shuffle his way around. Finally, however, the cold, slippery weather forced him to accept the suggestion from the management that he take a short vacation in a healthier part of the state. He went down to Moses' farm, stayed there for a week, and then, according to a letter from Colton to Huntington, returned: "Mr. Hopkins has just come into the office, and I am happy to say he is very much better . . ."

The improvement was, however, of short duration. A few months later rheumatism again laid him low. The attack was the most severe one yet and it became obvious that unless something drastic was done he would not live long. Thus he made no protest when his associates suggested a trip to the warm, dry climate of Arizona. A special company train was arranged and a party of friends selected to accompany him on his journey. The train left San Francisco on March 22, 1878, with Hopkins comfortably settled in a special coach, a warm stove by his bed to make his passage as pleasant and easy as possible.

Seven friends were with him: Dr. A. B. Nixon; S. S. Montague, chief engineer of the Central Pacific Railroad; his brother Moses; two Sacramento friends, Benjamin Welch and J. R. Watson; Arthur Brown; and a young physician friend from San Francisco whose name, oddly enough, none of the newspapers revealed. The second day out the train passed through the San Joaquin Valley and the weather was so warm and sunny that Mr. Hopkins was able to sit up all day and to eat with relish. As the train mounted the Caliente mountain range, the weather became very cold and windy and with this change, Hopkins again had a severe rheumatic attack. It was so bad that the train was forced to slow down to a snail's pace in order to ease the bumps and sways in Hopkins' coach. Reaching Los Angeles, the party was dismayed to discover that the winter storm was raging there too, so, despite the discomfort of travel in such weather, they pushed on into the San Bernardino Valley and eventually got out of the storm at Colton. They remained there for a few days. As soon as Hopkins had recovered some of his strength, the train continued on again. This time it went over the newly completed Sunset Route to their destination at Yuma, Arizona. After a few days in the hot dry climate of the desert, Hopkins seemed so much better that Dr. Nixon returned to Sacramento, feeling that his services were no longer required. He told the newspapers that he did not consider "Mr. Hopkins' case at all dangerous." *

But his diagnosis was obviously wrong. Early on the morning of March 29, while most of his friends were peacefully asleep, Mark Hopkins died in his bed. California and the West had lost one of their first citizens. It was Arthur Brown who found him in his death bed. It was the theory of the physician that the rheumatism had concentrated itself in his brain, causing the fatality.

* Sacramento Bee, March 29, 1878.

And so Mark Hopkins—of North Carolina, of the gold mines of California, of the railroad system of the West— "breathed his last on the banks of the Colorado. Among the old haciendas and under the burning sun of Yuma City, he pased away."

9

OBITUARIES AND POST-MORTEMS

On March 30, 1878, the day following Mark Hopkins' death, the Sacramento *Union* carried on its front page a two-column tribute that read in part:

A blow fell upon our city early yesterday. It came in the form of a telegram announcing the death of one of Sacramento's oldest and best friends, Mark Hopkins. He died at Yuma, Arizona territory, yesterday morning . . .

A telegram received by Hon. Leland Stanford yesterday reads as follows: "Yuma (Ariz), March 29,—8:10 A.M.—Mr. Hopkins died at 3:20 A.M. He had suffered considerably at intervals from his rheumatic pains since his arrival here Monday evening but for the last thirty-six hours had been comfortably free from pain and had rested better than previously. No alarming symptoms were manifest until within a few moments of his death. He passed away in sleep with no apparent pain or struggle. S. S. Montague."

On the receipt of the news in this city a mantle of gloom fell upon the community. Men passed in the streets with pale faces, grasped hands, and in subdued tones told the sad news "Mark Hopkins is dead." . . . In no place upon the face of the round earth were his virtues so widely known, so deeply realized, so broadly admired, as in Sacramento. It was his old home, the home of his triumphs, and the city fittingly clad herself in mourning . . . In the face of the death summons to such a man, mere detail as to his life would seem uncalled for, for his record being written in the history of our city, on the tablets of the State's progress, and engraved on the national annals is the story of the Construction of the great work of the age . . .

And so the tribute reads on, a heart-felt eulogy to a man who was known and admired by the citizens of California, and who was greatly responsible for the growth and prosperity of the Pacific Coast.

Other newspapers carried reports written in the same vein—respect for the man who had done so much in the West, grief over his loss, but with little or no biographical detail. The San Francisco *Daily Alta* commented on March 30: "By the death of Mark Hopkins, California loses one of her wealthiest millionaires and most competent and correct business men. Of all the Central Pacific Railroad magnates he was best known and had the least to do with the general public in reference to railroad business. He was a hard worker and it might almost be said that he had no enjoyment save in his work. He was quiet, unpretending, affable, and as popular as a millionaire could well be . . ."

The Oakland *Daily Times* of April 2 carried this partial notice on its front page: "The death of this notable and talented man is the first great blow that the original managers of the railroad system have ever received . . . Mr. Hopkins was a man of extraordinary ability and wonderful fertility of resources. . . . We differ with the living in regard to their actions and plans, but the grave closes all differences and all controversy."

Although the various large newspapers of California had sharp criticism for the manner in which the Central Pacific Railroad handled its finances and business transactions in the state, they all joined in common admiration and respect for the man Mark Hopkins. None could deny his talents, his energy, his business acumen, his genial disposition, his quiet manners, his gentility. His death was a genuine loss to the state as well as to the transportation industry which he had done so much to foster. These death notices are important to history because they point out the importance and fame that Mark Hopkins enjoyed during his life time— a fame and importance that have since been neglected by history. Yet these reports are more meaningful than merely as a record of public acclaim. Despite their generalities, they hold important keys to the questions under discussion. Not only are there inconsistencies within individual reports, but the factual material varies greatly from one paper to another. Some assign attributes of the New York Mark Hopkins to the railroad financier, consciously or unconsciously giving aid to the future perpetrators of fraud.

In these notices, one's attention is immediately attracted to the sincerity with which the newspapers describe Hopkins' character. Without exception they call attention to "his simplicity, integrity, and inflexibility. He was a symmetrical character according to its own type—true, just, merciful, tender. . . . He was himself and no one else, always and everywhere . . . He was a grand, plain, firm, just man . . . Rich or poor, he was the same. The acquirement of wealth did not soil his character. . . . Most of his noble acts and benefactions will never be known to us . . ." *

Such tributes befitted the tall bearded man from North Carolina who gave up his sweetheart and save his brother's

* Sacramento *Union*, April 2, 1878.

life, and who left the place of his birth and the friends and countryside he loved to accompany a thoughtless and reckless brother into the unknown West, who guarded his brother's secrets as his own and who continued to support, financially and morally, his brother to the day of his death. Such tributes are to a man who preferred a mountain log cabin to a mansion on Nob Hill, who avoided society, who lived by himself in peace and quiet, who devoted himself completely and whole-heartedly to the task of building a railroad line across the length and breadth of the West.

In marked contrast to these expressions of admiration are the blunt and prosaic statements at the end of the long obituaries: "The deceased leaves a wife, but no children." † "Mr. Hopkins leaves a wife and one adopted son." ‡ These pertinent facts are left to the end and are not elaborated. The Oakland, Los Angeles, and San Francisco papers do not even mention the wife and child, which is odd since most obituaries are expected to mention the survivors of the deceased. A man reputed to have been as tender-hearted and kind as Mark Hopkins would certainly have been known as a generous husband and loving father and his relations with his family would have excited comment. There is nothing in the papers to indicate that Mark Hopkins ever lived with a family in California, save that he had a wife. Such omission is doubly strange when we realize that up until the middle of 1876 there are frequent notices in the paper about the social activities of a "Mr. and Mrs. Mark Hopkins."

For instance, the Sacramento *Daily Record Union* for

† *Ibid.*, March 30, 1878.
‡ Sacramento *Bee*, March 29, 1878.

January 6, 1876, has the following social event recorded:
"After all the dreary, desolate snow-mantled Summit is not
considered a very bad place. On New Year's Eve, Mark
Hopkins, his wife and son, with a number of invited guests
came up from Sacramento and switched off at the Summit.
From Friday night until Monday morning their palace car
stood on the side tracks and the distinguished people enjoyed
themselves in the deep snow and among the icicles. They
brought a cook and had everything cozy, comfortable and
convenient. What a proof of the progress of the age is
offered. But the fact is that wealthy Californians are enabled
to leave their beautiful homes in the valley and safely spend
New Year's Eve among the storm clouds and snow drifts
on the Sierra Nevada and return home after having a jolly,
pleasant and happy time."

Such a party and such an account are hardly the kind
of social activity and public notoriety that a man remarkable
for his modesty was likely to be associated with. Nor is
such a holiday characteristic of a man suffering from rheumatism! The Mark Hopkins of fame and fortune lived
alone. He did not participate in social affairs. He gave no
parties, took no social trips. Nor did he have a wife or a
son to support and foster in society. The Mr. and Mrs.
Hopkins of these newspaper social notes are the couple who
were married in New York in 1854 while Mark Hopkins
of subsequent railroad fame was in a land office of the United
States Government in California. The newspapers accounts
are utterly inconsistent, sometimes assigning a wife and child
to the railroad director and at other times describing him
as a bachelor. Clearly the Mrs. Hopkins referred to in the

social note and in the obituaries is Mary Frances Sherwood Hopkins, wife of the Mark Hopkins of New York. The child is Timothy Nolan whom Mark Hopkins of New York and Michigan had brought up in his home as a son.

An equally important point about these obituaries is their uniform lack of exact biographical material. Surely California had a press sufficiently sophisticated and developed to accurately record the lives and careers of its famous men and women. Yet this press could give no details of the life of Mark Hopkins, a man whom it considered eminent in state affairs. This same press not only had no information of its own about Mark Hopkins; it had to go to the Society of California Pioneers in order to get material for the obituaries. But it has already been shown that Mark Hopkins of North Carolina did not come to California until after 1849—the deadline for all who could become members of the California Pioneers. Why the newspapers preferred to use the biographical data of this strictly local and amateur society instead of finding out the news from their own far superior sources of information can never be answered categorically. Either knowingly and under pressure from the railroad executives, or unknowlingly, they gave the wife and child of the Northerner to the Southerner and mixed and confused other facts in the lives of the two men.

In so doing, the papers made some fairly foolish errors. For instance, the Los Angeles *Republican* and the Oakland *Daily Times* both carried the statement that "Mr. Hopkins was a native of Jefferson County, New York, a grandson of the distinguished President Hopkins, and died at the age of sixty-three years." As it has been demonstrated, the railroad magnate was not born in Jefferson County, though his Yankee counterpart was. The Southerner, born in September of 1814, was sixty-three years old at the time of his death; his Yankee counterpart, born in September 1813, would have been sixty-four in March of 1878. But most interesting is the question of the relationship of the railroad magnate to Mark Hopkins, the educator and president of Williams College in Massachusetts. This Mark Hopkins was born in 1801 and was only eleven or twelve years older than the man described as "his grandson." Evidently this impossible situation was brought to the attention of the educator, who in a book of collected letters revealed his amusement over this false connection with the railroad executive. "Have you seen a notice of the death of Mark Hopkins, the millionaire of California?" the letter asks. "One paper sent me said that he was my son. He was a distant relative, though I never saw him. Another paper said he was sixty-some years old and my grandson."

Perhaps the newspapers were only careless when they made the railroad man and the educator relatives, but it would appear that a deliberate attempt was made to relate them, for indeed the Mark Hopkins of New York was a "distant relative" of the famous educator. They both belonged to the same family of Hopkins' which had settled in Connecticut in the first part of the seventeenth century, but neither was related in any way to the Hopkins family which immigrated to America in the middle of the eighteenth century and from which the railroad capitalist was descended. Even *Time Magazine* in its October 19, 1936, issue has occasion to correct the misconception. In its account

The old Central Pacific Railroad as it crossed the wild and rugged Sierras. The Indians and many of the "Mountaineers" had never seen a train before.

Hopkins mausoleum in City Cemetery, Sacramento. Here are buried Mark, Moses, Ezra Augustus, and Samuel A. Hopkins. The inscriptions state that the first three were brothers and that Samuel was their nephew.

Henry Treichler home, built in 1875 and still standing at 1926 H Street in Sacramento. A lonely bachelor, Mark Hopkins spent many happy hours here as the the guest and close friend of Mr. and Mrs. Treichler.

Three pieces from an eight-piece set of parlor furniture which Mark Hopkins gave the Treichlers in 1875 when their new home was completed.

of the Hopkins Centenary at Williams College, the magazine added: "No kin to Williams' Mark Hopkins was California Capitalist Mark Hopkins, who helped build the Southern Pacific Railroad and for whom San Francisco's Hotel is named."

Other strange and perplexing relatives were announced by the various dailies as belonging to the railroad magnate. Thus the Sacramento *Union* said: "A large connection of kindred, both here and in the East, are bereaved by his loss." The Sacramento *Bee* wrote of two nieces, "recent arrivals from England, who were under his protection." Another paper lists among the family mourners "Mr. Crittenden, of St. Louis, brother-in-law to Mr. Hopkins, and with him his wife, Mrs. Hopkins' sister, and their two daughters." Another mentions Mr. Crittenden, but not his wife, and without daughters. This gentleman never again appears in any of the biographies of Mark Hopkins, nor, more important, does his name occur in any of the records of the settlement of the estate. Presumably the "two nieces from England" were the girls that were referred to as the daughters of Mr. Crittenden, although in one report the family is from England, in another from St. Louis, and in yet another from Massachusetts. These Crittendens would seem to have been related to the Mark Hopkins of New York, but their origins and connections are indeed vague and inconsistent in the several newspaper accounts.

When the Sacramento *Bee*, a newspaper heavily influenced by the opinions and wishes of the railroad executives, made its announcement of the family relationships and the survivors, its list became more or less recognized as the official one. On April 5, 1878, the *Bee* announced that the survivors of the capitalist were "two brothers, Moses and Samuel, also a wife and an adopted son. Moses Hopkins at present resides near the mouth of Bear River, Sutter County, and is engaged in farming . . . Samuel Hopkins is at present residing in the state of Michigan and has three sons. Two of these, William and Edward, are married and reside in San Francisco, the latter having been Deputy Treasurer of the railroad company under Mark Hopkins. A third resides at Sheridan . . . and is named Orin Hopkins. He is also married and is agent for the company at that point." This list does not include any nieces or brothers-in-law. Yet a week before, the same paper had credited Mark Hopkins with "two nieces, under his protection," and had neglected to include nephews. Such inconsistencies cannot be accepted as mere journalistic carelessness. No, it must be assumed that within a week after the death of Mark Hopkins the plot to grasp his fortune from his legitimate heirs had already been formulated. Within a week it had been decided who was to receive and who was not to receive. Moses, of course, was a brother, and he therefore had to be included. Then there was the wife of the New York Hopkins and her adopted son who were to be designated as the chief beneficiaries.

How was Hopkins' death accepted by his railroad partners? Curiously enough, there were few reports in the papers on the reactions of the railroad company and its officials to the loss of one of its most significant members. Undoubtedly there were some in the company offices who were saddened by the loss; others, however, may have found good reason for relief. In the very year of Hopkins' death, the finances of the Central Pacific Railroad were under serious scrutiny by state and federal government officials. The company itself was not in public favor; its monopolistic practices and ruthless acquisition of land and property had won it few friends among the general public of California; its bonds were of dubious value; and the interest on government issues was overdue. Every dollar in credit and in cash was needed to pull the company through this difficult and critical period. Since few records had been kept of the most significant transactions in the early financing of the road, there was little that the government investigators could use as evidence. But if the company should fail in its commitments to its outstanding creditors, then the whole structure of the line would collapse. At this point it was important to have some cash assets and free shares available with which to pay some of the outstanding loans. With such resources the rest of the shares and bonds and debit accounts of the company could be sustained. The death of Mark Hopkins made available huge assets in the form of cash, stocks, and bonds. The question in the minds of many of the officials must have been whether these assets could be used to tide the company over its critical financial time, or whether they would be withdrawn from the company, thus weakening the structure, perhaps beyond repair.

By following the accounts of the newspapers of the funeral and final burial of Hopkins, it is possible to appreciate some of the problems involved in creating one man out of two. On the day of his death the Sacramento *Bee* reported: "It is not known as yet whether the funeral will take place in this city or in San Francisco. Deceased has a lot in the cemetery here and . . . it is not improbable that he may be buried here." The following day the Sacramento *Union* was able to tell its readers: "Yesterday a dispatch from Edward Hopkins, a nephew of deceased, making inquiries as to the condition of Tenth St. to the Cemetery, led to the supposition that his burial here was contemplated. This, however, is not the case. His funeral will take place from his late residence, 731 Sutter St., San Francisco on April 1."

Though the funeral was held in San Francisco, it was not at Hopkins' former residence; instead, the Calvary Presbyterian Church was selected. Here a mammoth service, presided over by the Reverend Dr. Dwinell of Sacramento, was held before a crowded church of mourners. leading citizens of San Francisco and Sacramento were in attendance; every official of the railroad company and its subsidiaries was there; and the streets were lined with silent watchers as the procession left the church and headed for the Laurel Hill Cemetery. The procession was nearly a mile long; there were over a hundred hacks and more than forty private carriages following the hearse.

The casket was left in the vault of Judge Lorenzo Sawyer. Two years later it was removed to Sacramento and there placed in a mausoleum valued at 150,000 dollars and built by Mary Frances Hopkins on a lot in the City Cemetery. Here, too, were buried Ezra Augustus Hopkins and Samuel A. Hopkins and; when Moses Hopkins died in 1892, he also was buried here.

Now why was Mark Hopkins' final burial delayed for two years. If he really was a member of the New York

and Michigan family, why wasn't he buried in the Hopkins
family plot which Mark Hopkins had purchased in August
of 1865 on the occasion of the death of his brother Ezra
Augustus? This was the lot, mentioned in an earlier chapter, which, according to the Sacramento *Bee,* Edward Hopkins was inquiring into as a burial place for Mark Hopkins,
the railroad magnate. But the Southerner was not buried
in this family plot of the Northern Hopkins clan. Perhaps
this was too risky; better to wait a few years and then build
a new mausoleum and move the bodies of the New York
men into it, thus sealing the union of the North and the
South.

The inscriptions on this new mausoleum are also worthy
of study. Mark, Moses, and Ezra Augustus are made out to
be brothers, and Samuel A. is mentioned as a nephew of
the three. Yet there is proof that such a relationship could
not have existed among these men. In 1863 Moses Hopkins
testified to a ten-year friendship with Ezra Augustus Hopkins when the latter applied for his preemption claim.
Moses was not swearing as a relative, but as a friend. Several
decades later, it was convenient to make this same Ezra
Augustus his brother! As for Samuel, he was indeed the
son of Ezra's brother, Samuel Frederick, and thus was Ezra's
nephew; but he was no more related to Mark and Moses
Hopkins of North Carolina than these two were to Ezra.

There is yet one more significant point to be discussed
in connection with Hopkins' death and funeral. The California newspapers, as has been shown, devoted front-page
spreads to the death and the funeral. As Oscar Lewis has
remarked in his chapter on Hopkins, these obituaries "re-

tain to this day the ring of sincerity. Hopkins was unquestionably the best liked of the Big Four." * Despite the
shortcomings, the inconsistencies, the errors, known and unknown, the newspaper accounts were full and were carried
in all the papers of Sacramento, San Francisco, Los Angeles,
and Oakland. But there is no report in the Eastern newspapers.

One would assume that the sudden death of a man of
Mark Hopkins' stature would have elicited extensive treatment in the press of the nation. He was one of the wealthiest men of his day and one of the most influential in the
financial and transportation world. Yet not one newspaper
east of the Mississippi carried a notice of Hopkins' death—
the man whom Westerners were claiminng as a former resident of New York. The press of his native state and of the
city where he had been in business as a young man failed
to so much as mention his death. A careful search through
the newspapers of New York City, Boston, Springfield,
Washington, D.C., and Baltimore failed to reveal a single
line on the passing of the Central Pacific Railroad director.
His sudden death at Yuma and his extensive funeral in San
Francisco received no attention in the East, although these
events had received front-page coverage on the Pacific Coast.
It cannot be maintained that Eastern papers were not concerned with California affairs since all of them habitually
carried columns headed "News from San Francisco" or
"West Coast Notes." In these columns for the period from
March 30 to April 3, we read of such trivial news as the
sailing of the *City of Peking* from San Francisco, and that

* Oscar Lewis, *The Big Four*, Alfred A. Knopf, New York, 1938, p. 139.

George W. Abbott, a San Francisco broker, had absconded with funds from his company and had been duly arrested. People in the East were greatly concerned with the railroads and any news about the railroad companies and their owners and directors would naturally be of interest to them.

The explanation for the astonishing omission must be found elsewhere. It must first be found in the unwillingness to have the East, particularly the financiers and legislators of the East, know of the passing of an important railroad personage. Such news might prompt still more investigation into the affairs of the Central Pacific and might even fur-thur antagonize the public against the big monopolies in transportation. The second reason is even more obvious and pertinent: the New York relatives of the Mark Hop-kins whom they knew had died a few years before would indeed be surprised to read that he had died again! If they then realized that this man, who the papers asserted was their relative, was indeed a millionaire, they no doubt would have rushed to California to claim their legitimate shares of the vast estate. Such an onrush of heirs would have been calamitous. The news, therefore, of Hopkins' death had to be kept out of the Eastern papers, and the dispatchers of news from the West to the East seem to have cooperated fully in this silence. Huntington was living in New York at the time and could effectively prevent news from getting into the New York papers. He had been effective in far more complicated and difficult maneuverings.

In its own way, the absence of information about Hop-kins in the Eastern papers is as damning as the contradictory information in the Western dailies. Together, the omissions and the discrepancies serve as another clue to the controversy and indicate serious manipulation of public information. By concealing and by confusing, the conspirators hoped to erase the personalities of two men and create one personality. Though they were amazingly successful in their own time, the truth is at last emerging.

10

AN ESTATE VANISHES

Once Mark Hopkins was dead and buried, public interest revolved about the settlement of his estate. The Sacramento *Bee,* the paper most subject to the influence of the railroad men and the one in the best position to obtain the most accurate information, reported on April 5, 1878: "Several papers in this state have already assumed the responsibility of apportioning the estate of Mark Hopkins among his relatives and also give forth the impression that he died intestate. In these statements many wrong assertions have been made, and in order that they might be set right a representative of the *Bee* called on an old and intimate friend of the late Mark Hopkins and his family, and learned the following . . . As regards the matter of a will having been left by Mark Hopkins, it is positively known that he made all necessary arrangements for the disposal of his property after his death, but exactly what that disposition was, those who have a knowledge of it do not desire at present to make public, but in due time it will be published. It is difficult to estimate the total value of the estate, as much depends on future events for the value of the property to increase or even hold its present standard, but it is reckoned as being between $15,000,000 to $20,000,000."

Today, twenty million dollars is a great sum of money; in 1878 it was a staggering amount, and naturally people waited eagerly for the publication of the terms of Hopkins' will. Would he leave several million for civic improvements in Sacramento and San Francisco? What individuals would profit most? Would friends and business associates be remembered? What provisions had been made for his brother Moses?

The public was to wait in vain for the publication of the details. No will was ever published. In a few weeks the public learned, instead, that a mistake had been made. There was no will, after all, and Mark Hopkins had died intestate. The California Courts would be responsible for settling the estate. This sudden reversal was very odd and many people thought so at the time. Why, indeed, they asked, should the *Bee* have reported on good authority the existence of a will and then several weeks later have retracted their statement? Many thought then as many think now that it was ridiculous to assume that a man of Hopkins' wealth, position, and personal knowledge of money and finance should have been so careless, so unaware of his approaching death, so innocent of the ways in which a man's estate may be manipulated, as to have failed to write a will. If a Rockefeller or a DuPont were to die today and the newspapers to report the absence of a will, there would be a hue and cry of fraud and foul play. Millionaires, unless they are out of their minds, always make provision for the distribution of their wealth. It is ridiculous to pretend that Mark Hopkins really died intestate, as all the biographies claim. A man who was known in Sacramento and San

Francisco for his habit of picking up rusty nails and salvaging old metal was not the kind of man who would leave his millions to the disposition of strangers and of the courts.

The next point in the estate question is the appraisal of the estate made by E. H. Miller, A. J. Bryant, and B. B. Redding, who had been appointed the official appraisers by Judge Finn. The San Francisco *Daily Alta* published the report on its front page. The inventory showed that the debts due to the estate ran into the millions. The Western Development Company, the London and San Francisco Bank, the Central Pacific Railroad Company, and the Capital Savings Bank owed a total combined debt of $2,717,953.90. Among others, David D. Colton, Daniel Click, Edward W. Hopkins, and Leland Stanford were personally indebted to Mark Hopkins for an amount over $346,000. Then there was Mark Hopkins' share of real estate and property owned jointly with Huntington, Stanford, Crocker, Miller, and others. It was estimated at that time that "the estate was valued at $20,694,762.36." Later investigations have shown, however, that much property, both real and personal, had not been included in this original inventory. It is interesting to note that the Hopkins estate was singularly free of indebtness, in marked contrast to the three millions owed to it. No wonder his associates were concerned with how the estate would be settled—no wonder they personally saw to it that the estate would be settled in a manner favorable to them!

The third point in the estate settlement is concerned with Mary Frances Sherwood Hopkins, who on June 3, 1878, was granted Letters of Administration of the estate of Mark Hopkins by the Probate Court of San Francisco. Passing as the lawful wife of a man who had never married, and having worked for a year or so in his residence, she succeeded in becoming the lawful heir of Mark Hopkins, the railroad owner and director. According to California law, an applicant for Letters of Administration to a dead man's estate was required to notify the court of the names and addresses of all the heirs of the deceased. The court clerk then notified all the heirs of the place and time of hearings to determine how the estate would be settled. Mary Frances Hopkins listed but one heir with the Court—Moses Hopkins, although she must have known of the existence of seven other brothers and sisters who were living at that time in North Carolina. If, on the other hand, the Mark Hopkins who had died had really been, as all claimed, the Hopkins of New York State, she was guilty of not listing the brothers and sisters of that individual. Yet she chose to list only Moses.

Mary Frances administered the Hopkins estate for two years, but on or about August 26, 1881, she was removed (we do not know why), and Moses Hopkins was granted Letters of Administration on December 1, 1881. In his Letters of Application for the position, Moses made the same illegal omission as his predecessor. He failed to name his own brothers and sisters in North Carolina. He also deliberately lied to these brothers and sisters. Moses went so far as to tell one of his relatives who had written about Mark that Mark had recently died and had left a wife and nine children. In his letter, Moses lamented the passing of his brother and told his kinsmen that the entire estate had been left to Mark's immediate family and that no provision had been made for any of the North Carolina relatives. Naturally, the North Carolina family believed what Moses had written them; only years later did the nieces and nephews of Mark Hopkins, hearing rumors of what had happened in California, begin to investigate the settlement of the estate.

Moses' application was granted, even though he was legally ineligible to act as an administrator. California law stated that anyone convicted of a crime was automatically prohibited from serving as an administrator of an estate.

Moses not only concealed the names of the rightful heirs; he also concealed much of the property, real and personal, of the estate. In the fall of 1883 Moses applied to the Superior Court of the City and County of San Francisco for a final decree of settlement of the accounts and distribution of the estate of Mark Hopkins. On November 1 of that year, more than five years after the death of the railroad magnate, the court finally issued its decree of distribution. This decree is the legal instrument which disposed of Hopkins' wealth and property and which attorneys have since studied and found void on numerous counts.

The decree stated "that the administrator rendered a full account and report of his administration," but this was manifestly untrue. Many of the stocks listed among Hopkins' personal property were non-existent at the time of his death, notably the stocks of five railroad companies which had previously been absorbed by the Central Pacific Railroad Company. When the Big Four consolidated its many railway holdings into the corporation known as the Central Pacific Railroad Company, the stocks of the individual lines were exchanged for stocks in the super-corporation. Mark Hopkins owned hundreds of shares of Central Pacific stock, valued by the courts at $24,940,597.29, yet none of this stock was listed in the decree of distribution. No official accounting has ever been made of these millions of dollars' worth of stock, and one can only assume that they were utilized by the remaining directors of the company to support their own financial positions. Other shares were also omitted. Cash on hand, stocks, bonds, and other personal property amounting to another twenty-five million was not accounted for in the purported decree of distribution. This included stocks in six railroad companies, in steamship lines, mining companies, banks, insurance firms, and road companies. Nor were the household furnishings, the real estate, live stock, and debts due included. A comparsion of the published inventory (which in itself was incomplete) of the estate and the actual decree of distribution points up the many discrepanies and outright omissions. Almost fifty million dollars' worth of property was never legally disposed of by the California courts. Mary Frances and Moses shared unjustly in the reported wealth of the estate, but who shared the much larger amounts that were never reported? The disappearance of this fifty million dollars is one of the most fascinating, as well as nefarious, aspects of the Mark Hopkins controversy.

The failure of both Moses and Mary Frances to notify the clerk of the court of the existence and place of residence of the lawful heirs of the North Carolina Mark Hopkins alone invalidates the decree. This decree names "Mrs. Mary Frances Sherwood-Hopkins the only person interested in said Estate except said Administrator." Yet

further along in the same decree another name is referred
to—that of Samuel F. Hopkins, the oldest brother of the
Mark of New York and father of Edward, William, Orin,
and "Young" Mark Hopkins. Samuel, of course, was no
more entitled to a share of the magnate's fortune than was
Mary Frances, but his presence was necessary to those who
were handling the confusion between the name of a Mark
Hopkins of New York and the estate of the railroad director and builder from North Carolina. When the California
courts recognized Samuel F. as a brother of Mark Hopkins,
they should also have recognized his sons as nephews of the
deceased man. Four sons were living at the time—most of
them in the vicinity of San Francisco—but there is no mention of these heirs in the decree of distribution. Even if the
estate of the New York Hopkins had been the one under
consideration, these nephews should have been noted, and
since they were not, the decree is subject to question on
this one point alone.

Another fallacy in the decree is that Mary Frances was
granted three-fourths of the alleged estate. California law
in 1878 provided that the widow of a deceased man who
died intestate was entitled to but one-half of the decedent's
estate, yet Mary Frances, posing as the wife of the millionaire, was granted three-fourths.

On April 5, 1879, Samuel joined with Moses and Mary
Frances in making out an indenture assigning to Collis P.
Huntington, Charles Miller, Albert Gallatin, and W. R. S.
Foyle all the business property and assets that had formerly
belonged to Mark Hopkins as a partner in Huntington,
Hopkins & Company. This deed defines in minute detail

business property in San Francisco and Sacramento that had been owned by Huntington & Hopkins before Mark's death and assigns all of it to the new firm of Huntington & Hopkins Company, composed of the four men mentioned.

On September 4, 1879, Samuel Frederick and Moses Hopkins signed an agreement with Mary Frances whereby they permitted the Court in its final disposition of the estate to distribute the entire amount of real estate to Mrs. Hopkins. On March 13, 1880, this agreement was formalized in a deed stating: "Samuel F. Hopkins and Moses Hopkins, heirs at law of Mark Hopkins deceased . . . grant, bargain, sell, convey, unto Mary Frances Hopkins of the City and County of San Francisco and to her heirs and assigns forever all of their right title and interest to and in all real estate of which the said Mark Hopkins did seize and possess situated lying and being within the State of Califronia, the interest of each in said real estate being an undivided eighth part which they hereby severally convey." *

The agreements between the three Hopkins'—Mark's brother, a woman claiming to be Mark's wife, and a non-relative of the same last name—are both void, even as is the decree of distribution. The San Francisco Court did ratify such a deed, even when the real estate is not described. Hopkins was known to have owned vast amounts of land in San Francisco itself, and in Alameda, San Joaquin, Contra Costa, Sacramento, Placer, Nevada, Sierra, Yuba, Butte, Tehama, Stanislaus, Merced, Fresno, Tulare, Kern, San Bernardino, San Mateo, Santa Clara, Calaveras, Solano,

* Vol. 23, p. 525, Deed Records of the Court of San Mateo, State of Calif.

Napa, and Yolo counties, yet not one acre of all this real estate is defined or located in the deed.

A telling detail in these contracts reveals that Moses had some slight conscience when he gave Mary Frances only "one undivided eighth part" of the real estate. He had seven brothers and sisters living at that time and he may have thought that eventually the other seven-eighths of the property could be given to the other seven rightful heirs. Later writers have tried to justify this "one-eighth" clause. For instance, B. B. Redding's highly suspect *Sketch* says that the Hopkins family included seven brothers and two sisters and thereby hopes to explain the one-eighth clause. Redding's statements were verified by testimony given by Timothy Hopkins, but it has been proved in the fourth chapter of this book that only six sons and two daughters were born to Mark Hopkins of Henderson and St. Clair. Two sons had died before attaining manhood, so that in reality the family consisted of six children. Redding was hard put to it to justify the one-eighth deed for he not only included Moses as a member of the New York Hopkins family but he neglected to tell his readers that Ezra Augustus, William, and Augustus Hopkins had already died. Recent biographers have not taken Redding's or Timothy Hopkins' family statements seriously, but apparently they have overlooked the significance of Moses' real estate deed— a deed that definitely indicates the existence of other close relatives.

Shortly after Moses and Samuel Frederick executed these deeds, Moses acquired Samuel Frederick's interest in the estate. It is not known how this was accomplished. Prob-

ably a cash settlement was made. It is noteworthy that
when Moses Hopkins died in 1892 he left the major portion
of his fortune to "his nephews," and to their children, all
descendents of Samuel Frederick Hopkins.

All the foregoing serves to point out the illegalities which
were permitted to stand in the decree of distribution of
Mark Hopkins' estate. Millions of dollars' worth of stock,
real estate, and other property was omitted from the settlement. The definition of heirship was vague and incorrect.
No mention was made of the seven brothers and sisters of
Moses and Mark Hopkins. In fact, lawyers have found
thirteen legal errors in the decree. The documents, personalities, and circumstances that contributed to the settlement
of the estate were obviously part of a careful plan to deceive
the courts and to commit fraud.

Moses Hopkins died a rich man in 1892, taking a seven-
eighths interest of his share of his brother's estate with him to
the grave. As far as has been determined, the seven-eighths
share belonging to the brothers and sisters of Mark Hopkins
in North Carolina and reserved by Moses in his deed to
Mary Frances has never been accounted for either in the
settlement of Moses' estate or that of Mark Hopkins. What
happened to the missing seven-eighths of the real property
inherited by Moses Hopkins is yet another mystery in the
case. Old acquaintances of Moses have said that he was
delirious for days before he died, that he raved incessantly
about his brother Mark, that he groaned aloud thinking of
his sins, and that he pleaded with his wife and friends to
get a lawyer so he could make a proper will, leaving his
fortune to his true brothers and sisters. These same ac-

quaintances relate, however, how Edward Hopkins was constantly at the bedside of the dying man and refused to grant any of his requests. In fact, they say it was rumored in San Francisco that Edward Hopkins and other railroad men forced Moses to sign a will which they had had prepared for him. His final will authenticates the influence of Edward Hopkins, since he was appointed one of the executors of the estate and was granted large sums for himself, his wife, his children, his brothers, and his nephews and nieces.

This raises another question about the heirship that was stated in the decree. It implies that Mary Frances and Moses Hopkins were the only two heirs interested in the Hopkins money. Yet Moses Hopkins left substantial sums to Edward and "Young" Mark, as well as to their wives and children and to the children of Orin Hopkins. These individuals were very much alive at the time of the railroad magnate's death and if they were nephews as Moses claimed, they should have been listed as heirs of Mark Hopkins and should have received original settlements at that time.

The second claimant to the Hopkins estate, Mary Frances Sherwood Hopkins, enjoyed her great wealth for only a decade, but during that brief time she achieved great notoriety and received considerable public attention. As one of America's wealthiest widows, her comings and goings attracted constant notice in society columns throughout the country. She had a mad passion for architecture and interior decoration and once the Hopkins millions were in her bank account, she indulged her whims. Her first act was to complete the mansion on Nob Hill, begun by Mark shortly before his death. The mansion turned out to be a huge castle-like structure with towers, turrets, gables, high-paneled ceilings, and other extravagant appointments. These became the laughing stock of San Francisco. But Mrs. Hopkins did not remain in San Francisco long to hear the laughter. She went back to Great Barrington, Massachusetts, where she promptly embarked on what the newspapers chose to call a "building spree." Her building passion found expression in New York City, Block Island, and Methuen, Massachusetts, where she built a series of grand residences.

In the process of her building and decorating, Mary Frances met a young interior decorator, Edward T. Searles, and to the horror of her adopted son, Timothy, and to the surprise and humor of the world, she married the unknown furniture enthusiast who was more than twenty years her junior. The marriage broke the strong bonds between the son and mother, and thereafter the two rarely communicated. Timothy, who managed Mrs. Hopkins' financial affairs in California, felt that Searles was little more than a fortune-hunter and argued against his mother's marriage until she forbade him to mention the subject again. Relations were strained, though Timothy continued to act as her financial manager. When Mary Frances died on July 26, 1891, no one, least of all Timothy, was prepared for her final act of hostility. The woman had completely disinherited her foster son and had left her entire estate to Edward Searles. No charities, no servants, no relatives, no friends received a penny of her fortune. Timothy, as was to be expected, contested the will, charging that it had been made "under undue influence." Two months after her death, Mary Frances was still prominent in the newspapers. The trial over her will took place in Salem, Massachusetts, and the courthouse was jammed with curious spectators eagerly waiting to hear Searles' account of his romance with the heiress of the railroad millions. On the first day it became evident that Searles was nervous and hesitant at disclosing the details of his marriage. When court adjourned that evening, he instructed his attorneys to make an out-of-court settlement with Timothy. Whatever sum was finally agreed upon is not known. The Boston *Globe* stated that it was "between eight and ten millions," but Timothy is quoted as saying that "he was given twelve million dollars in a settlement to keep closed lips on the subject of the Mark Hopkins fortune."

Searles retained, of course, a large bulk of the fortune, including much railroad stock, but he retired from public view and never interfered with the affairs of the companies which were earning him his wealth. Timothy continued active in railroad affairs, although he never attained a prominent position in the Southern Pacific. Like his "step" cousins, Edward, Orin, and "Young" Mark, he was a treasurer for the railroad companies and served as an administrator for many years. True to his promise, Timothy never publicly revealed his knowledge of what happened at the time of Mark Hopkins' death, but there is evidence that he did submit to pressure once in court and frequently in private company.

When the settlement of the Hopkins estate was questioned by a California Court in 1924, Timothy Hopkins, along with Emily Benedict Hopkins, Moses' wife, and George W. Bray, an intimate friend of Moses from Sutter

County, were ordered to give testimony in open court. Judge Peter J. Shields of the Superior Court of Sacramento ordered that the depositions of these three persons be taken and further that they be recorded by the court clerk. The judge's orders were not executed—no parts of any of the three depositions were ever recorded in the state court records as ordered. The statute books still testifies that the order was given: "It is further ordered that the testimony of Timothy Hopkins be taken before W. H. Pyburn, a Notary Public in and for the city and County of San Francisco . . . It is further ordered that said depositions be returned to the county clerk of the County of Sacramento, State of California, when taken." The order was given on October 23, 1924, and on December 29 of that same year the Minute Docket of the Superior Court records that Judge John F. Pullen again "advised orders that said testimony be written up and returned to this court." * But none of the testimony of the case has been preserved. The entire proceedings are missing from the court, and only the brief notices cited prove that they ever took place. Indeed it is known that the testimony was given to the Notary Public and returned to the court clerk, for Mr. George Bray, in letters to the heirs, frequently asked what happened to the testimony which he gave to the court. Nobody knows where it went or why it was not filed—making one more mysterious circumstance pointing to trickery and extra-legal action.

One of the spectators at the hearings, however, did take notes and has related what happened. This woman was a

* Register of Actions 59, page 66.

descendant of the New York Hopkins family who had been
working on family history in California, and she herself
was so convinced that her ancestor was not the railroad
capitalist that she willingly gave her shorthand transcription
to the North Carolina heirs. The notes on Timothy's testimony are very revealing, and one can readily understand
why they were not filed in the records as ordered:

Q. Was Mark Hopkins, railroad magnate, ever married?
A. Not that I know of.
Q. Wasn't Mary Frances Sherwood Hopkins his wife?
A. She was not.
Q. Why was she in his home at the time he died?
A. She was the head servant or housekeeper.
Q. How long was she in the home of the railroad magnate?
A. Only a few months prior to his death.
Q. How did she secure employment in the home?
A. Through Moses, with whom she had a love affair. Moses
   deserted her and Mark gave her employment through sym-
   pathy.
Q. But why would Mark be responsible for Moses?
A. Don't know why—but it was common knowledge that
   he assumed all responsibility for him from the day they
   set foot on California soil until the day of his death in
   1878.
Q. Did you stay in the home of the railroad magnate?
A. No. Mother (Mary Frances) and I had a little cottage and
   she commuted daily to her work.
Q. Why do you call Mary Frances mother?
A. She reared me from a small boy.
Q. Did she legally adopt you?
A. Yes. After I was twenty-one for legal purposes.
Q. But how did you come into possession of the Hopkins
   millions?

A. It was given me by Mother (Mary Frances) and Moses Hopkins.

Q. But why did you later sue your foster mother?

A. I was not satisfied with the millions that she and Moses had given me. I felt that she owed me more liberal shares of the estate, since she had obtained it under false pretense. I had as much right to it as she.

Q. Did you win the suit when you entered suit against her?

A. No. It never went that far. We compromised.

Q. But there was no will found—how do you know he left one?

A. I know he left a will.

Q. Did you read it?

A. No. I was granted permission to read it—but for personal reasons I did not care to know its contents.

Timothy Nolan Hopkins died in 1936, and with his death the last actual witness and party to the Mark Hopkins fraud passed away. Now evidence must be evolved from documentary sources, since the human witnesses consistently refused to reveal the truth about the settlement. Scattered memories and second-hand accounts remain to point to the existence of gross deception and fraudulent distribution. In most cases these personal records are substantiated by documentary material, pieced together after years of arduous research.

Even as Mark Hopkins and his estate vanished quickly, so the documents and records and witnesses to the fraud have vanished. But the intrinsic wealth of the estate is still intact. The truth about the man and his work remains for those who will search for it.

Mark Hopkins' fortune evaporated by the relatively simple expedient of assigning the North Carolina capitalist's property to the relatives of the Hopkins of New York. Sufficient proof now exists to establish the identity and careers of the two Mark Hopkins' of Sacramento and San Francisco. Once this proof is accepted, the rest of the plot begins to unravel. Further than the misappropriation of the estate is the continuing mystery of what happened to that large portion of Mark Hopkins' fortune that was never listed and never distributed. Despite the passage of years, this vast property still exists and still remains to be distributed to the Hopkins' heirs.

11

SUMMARY AND CONCLUSIONS

In the course of digging up the facts for this book and presenting the arguments and the interpretations, it has been
obvious that much remains to be checked, many links must
still be found, many records must still be verified. Yet the
basic information on which a new understanding of the
Mark Hopkins Controversy can be founded is here. From
these facts it is evident that attorneys and judges can reach
a new decision and a new, fairer, more complete distribution of the fortune of the railroad magnate. Perhaps then
Mark Hopkins will have a museum, a library, a university,
an art gallery named after him, instead of just a hotel. Like
the other members of the Big Four, he will take his rightful
place in American transportation and financial history.

It has been established that there were two contemporary
Mark Hopkins'—that one came from a family residing in
North Carolina and that the other came from a family native
to New York State and later residents of Michigan. These
two families were not related to each other, except in so
far as the members of their family connived to make them
relatives. The link that ties Mark Hopkins the railroad
builder and transportation genius to the family in North
Carolina is his brother Moses, whose existence has never

been doubted, whose relation to Mark Hopkins has never been contested, and whose early manhood in North Carolina has in this volume been fully explored and revealed.

This volume has also shown the way in which Moses Hopkins was associated with Ezra Augustus Hopkins, one of the sons of the Hopkins family of New York and Michigan. These two men were friends, as the Land Office preemption claim clearly and without reservations states. Yet the courts permitted these two men to become brothers when the estate of Mark Hopkins was up for settlement. The courts also permitted the deceased Mark Hopkins to have a wife—woman he was supposed to have married in 1854 at a time when other records show him to have been in California, 3600 miles from the scene of the marriage. Only in recent times has it become possible for a man to marry in New York one day and several days later be in California before a government official. In 1854 it was humanly impossible to be on both sides of the continent during a week's time, a month's time, a three-month's time. Clearly, two men had to be alive, each with the name of Mark Hopkins, in order for one to be married and the other to be present at a government bureau during the same short period.

Fraud enters the picture when we examine the United States Census for 1870. Here we find that an unknown hand has changed the essential facts about Mark Hopkins' personal and real property. Why such a change if not to establish the fact that the Mark Hopkins of New York had a fortune large enough in 1870 to permit his family to claim the fortune of Mark Hopkins, the North Carolina native and the builders of the Central Pacific Railroad? It has been shown that the change in the United States Census has been of recent date, that it was not an error made at the time of the taking of the census. Such a change could have been made only by persons most anxious to keep the true facts from public scrutiny.

Fraud is transparent in the newspaper accounts, the conflicting biographical reports, the denial of a will. Here we find confusion, inconsistency, and omissions that can be explained in no other way.

Omissions also characterize the inventory of the estate. Great areas of land, hundreds of shares of valuable corporation stocks, numerous holdings in smaller companies, and debts and accounts are willfully withheld from the inventory of a vast estate. Some fifty million dollars that were unaccounted for are still in need of final and complete legal disposition.

The double image, created from the portraits and the lives of two men, has now been clarified. Two men stand out as the distinct individuals they most certainly were in their own lifetimes. These two men deserve better of history; their families deserve better of justice. There is no longer and justification for a "Mark Hopkins Controversy." The evidence presented in this volume resolves it.

Copyright Applied For,
By Edwin A. Sherman.

The raising of the American Flag at Sutter's Fort, California, by Captain John A. Sutter.

HISTORY OF MARK HOPKINS WITH RELATIONSHIPS TO THE CONTRACT AND FINANCE COMPANY

Mark Hopkins, the great Southerner, became President of the Contract and Finance Company in the early years of "Railroad Construction"—and maintained this position until the time of his decease on March 29, 1878. Through this gigantic construction company, he was able to see the great overland chain of railroads become a reality. The Central Pacific Was The First.

Many subsidiaries accompanied this great feat in its manifold achievements and accomplishments which projected in manifold manner great means of transportation by land and sea.

Hopkins, the great Southerner, arrived in California shortly after the mad gold rush had reached its zenith. Then taking up from the Argonauts, growth in "Railroads"—prominence and eminence in all fields of industrial expansion became synonymous.

Next in the progression of railroad controls—arose a great financial arrangement with the United States Government. Negotiations with reference to the Federal Land Grants and Patents which had been granted to build, construct, and finance the building of the Great Central Pacific Railroad and all its subsidiaries—had not proven to a great degree of satisfaction in its economical digest to the nation as a whole. Something had to be done to promote the financial power to push forward further constructions; the barren soils had to be populated with buildings to house the homesteaders; build and erect buildings, in beautiful structures of architectural designs—continue the furtherance of Spanish Culture plus the many other nationalities which migrated to "THE GOLDEN SHORES OF CALIFORNIA!"

Gigantean, enormous, and inordinate construction works which had overcome the wild and rugged Sierras—did not embrace adequate support, power, and progression—: "Something had to happen for some great 'FINANCIERS TO TAKE OVER THE RESPONSIBILITY OF THE BOND SYSTEM' or else the entire nation would end in one of the greatest financial predicaments ever known to a civilized world." A catastrophe, sudden calamity, misery and misfortune seemed inevitable.

But to whom could "The Federal Government Turn?"

"Mark Hopkins supplied the sufficient requirements!"— He had gained control over mint productions in San Francisco—(where now stands what is known as the "Old Mint Building"); at this contemporary existence in the life of the great "Carolinian" the foreseeable future would unveil unfoldments to gain a monopolistic control over other mint locals and designated places throughout the civilized world.

Due to space in one volume book—it is answering all requirements of an adaptation to the end in view: That Mark Hopkins, of Randolph County, North Carolina—did assume the following obligations and carried them through to a logical conclusion.

1—Mark Hopkins, as an individual, unaided and unassisted retired the "GOLD BOND SYSTEMS" which built the "OVERLAND CHAINS OF RAILROADS"—and supplied the "Financial Backings" through the "Money Exchangers" for every giant corporation in the United States of America!

2—When the assembling in the structure of the Central Pacific Railroad had reached completion—it marked the culmination of a movement that began before the years of 1830 —perhaps much longer than that—when the first locomotives may have been brought to America. (It is still debatable.) Not over a third of a century had elapsed from the opening of the first section of the Baltimore and Ohio, until the breaking of ground for the Central Pacific at Sacramento in 1863 had reached completion.

In a short duration of the time element—over thirty thousand miles of railroad had been constructed in the United States. At the dawn of 1870, over fifty two thousand miles of line had been built and in full operation. Due to this great expansion in the "rails"—it was a pronounced fact that it could be credited as the contributor to the rapid expansion, growth and all forms of progressive development in the American nation.

3—Few Historians will refer to the days when men sat around on nail kegs in the old Huntington and Hopkins Hardware establishment, making railroading their main point of interest and the main topic of conversation. Neither will a single historian admit that Mark Hopkins was the propeller which inspired the emotional flames which Theodore Judah adapted in his journey in the manifold obstacles that he encountered during his surveys, and by the inspirational pathway which he had to travel in order to cope with adversities.

Mark Hopkins was the first to discuss the feasibility of Judah's surveys. He was the first to endorse Judah when a meeting was held in Sacramento to discuss plans for the great project which resulted in an organization. Leland Stanford, Collis Potter Huntington, Charles Crocker attended the meeting, along with others, but, irrespective a financial support had to be guaranteed for the surveys.

4—Leland Stanford, Charles Crocker, E. H. Miller, Jr., and many other seekers of fame and fortune, had joined in with the capitalist of the "Nation" in the construction of the Sacramento and Placerville Railroad. This was the first Railroad in California and early histories report that it made its first successful run in 1854.

It was at this time, Mark Hopkins of Lockport, New York, was assigned position as Treasurer, and E. H. Miller Jr., was given the position in the capacity as Secretary.

Miller and Hopkins were operating a wholesale grocery establishment at 160 Jay Street—had been very successful as merchants, established a good reputation in business, and had gained the respectability of their patrons throughout Sacramento and its locals.

Around September of 1854 Mark Hopkins sold out to Miller—and sailed for New York to marry his boyhood sweetheart, Mary Frances Sherwood. He and Miller had decided to sever their relationship as direct partners. As a result—Mark Hopkins established a grocery store in his own name—and acquired what was known as a small fortune in those days (around thirty eight thousand dollars). However, as time marched on—he ventured more and more in the railroad progression. He was treasurer, and could see great possibilities in the future venture and speculative enterprise.

Mary Frances, the wife whom he married September 20, 1854—urged him to follow in sequent order with his investors —which would transcend any capital stock owner in the original corporation. She was a very cold blooded monetary creature—and all the love she carried in life was for "earthly possessions!". Apparently, and judging by the United States Population Census Schedule for the year ending 1870—he was reduced to poverty. (This was the U. S. Census Report —which was erased and falsified in the personal and real property to appear in numerals which would be comparative to the "Partners" of the "Railroad Magnate, Mark Hopkins, of Randolph County, North Carolina.") (See Page 159.)

5—Judging from the factual data which I have dedicated my life in the great and potent endeavor to uncover the true biography of Mark Hopkins, son of Edward Hopkins and Hannah Crow Hopkins—a progenitor of the ancestral lineage from Bedding County, Virginia, and North Carolina—. "The North Carolina, Mark Hopkins emassed the greatest fortune known to American History, or to our contemporaneous existence—has been established immovably and firmly, ordained and enacted for preeminence, as an unparalleled contributor to civilization—plus one of the civilized world's greatest philanthropists: Yet he is now buried in the Sacramento Cemetery—unidentified and unclaimed."

6—However, since writing the first issue of "Controversial Mark Hopkins—The Great Swindle of American History"— I was fortunate enough to obtain through Sacramento's oldest "Pioneer Funeral Home"; Clark, Booth, & Yardley, a mortuary report of his "Nativity"—which read: "N. C." (The "C" had been erased and the letter "Y" written over it— with ink shades of a much later date. The "C" still was clear to the visible eye when one looked at it closely—even without a magnifying glass.)

7—The Brother, Moses's report reported his "NATIVITY" as "HOPKINS." This was the small country crossroad "VILLAGE"—just a short distance from the scene of action in Wake County, North Carolina, the locale in which he stole the horse. It still bears that name, with little change of growth since 1845—at the time Moses Hopkins led away the grey "MARE" horse from Jermiah Miles, a "Neighbor."

8—Stealing the "Mare" herein referred to, led to the basis upon which the fraudulent scheme was perpetrated by his surviving partners, their associations and affiliation. Horse stealing in those pioneer days was punishable by death. The one who helped the escapee was considered as guilty as if he had performed and committed the offense himself.

9—Mark Hopkins, was never identified by any Federal Census Report—because the names of the residues in a family unit were not mandatory until the 1850 enumeration.

10—When he reached California March 24, 1851, he and Moses joined a nephew in Yuba City, whose name appeared in the Federal Enumeration Population as a "Native of North Carolina." He was engaged in the mining industry, and had attained a remarkable degree of success. Simultane-

ously, his "Uncle Mark" stepped into the glamorous venture:
—"I WILL TEACH THIS NEPHEW OF MINE HOW
TO REACH FAME'S HILL!"—so said Mark Hopkins!
From that day on he accepted his fate: "Comparative to
Fanny in the 'Tale of Two Cities' by the famous English
Author, Charles Dickens." "I will accept my destiny—just
as a ship that sails on the sea—and, destined for some foreign
port. I will never turn back. I can visualize my foreseen
future. I am going to build an 'EMPIRE' out of this wil-
derness. The deplorable South is suffering desperately by
'High Tariff' which the 'North' has imposed upon us!"

11—It was not until the "STATE RAILROADS" had
collapsed because of the lack of adequate financial aids—that
Mark Hopkins took the "Railroad Study Under Serious Consideration!" When the experiment of Pennsylvania, Massachusetts, North Carolina, Georgia, Indiana, Michigan, and
Illinois tried their experiment—after the panic of 1837, going
in debt in exceess of $5,000,000, was forced to sell out for a
loss. Because of the manifold lengthy series of misdirected
endeavors, characterized by all forms of corruption, misman-
agement, and political imcompetence, Mark Hopkins decided
to use his private fortune—which he had acquired from the
mining industry in California and Nevada to save the railroad
industry, promotional value for civilization and the growth
of the United States of America and assume the responsibility of the "BOND SYSTEM"—which saved the railroad
system of America.

12—There is a great difference in the discrimination of a
"STOCKHOLDER" and "BONDHOLDER." The fol-
lowing is exemplar:

Difference between bondholders and stockholders.

As the bond is the written promise of the railroad company to pay to the one entitled thereto, according to its terms, the holder of such bond is a creditor of the issuing railroad company.

The bondholders are creditors of the railroad company; the stockholders are members of the company that owes the money to the bondholders. The bondholders are entitled to demand payment of their bonds and interest of the railroad company; the stockholders are members of the company that must pay the bondholders.

When the assets of a railroad company are finally distributed upon a winding up of its affairs, the bondholders and the other creditors are first paid in full, according to their respective priorities, before the stockholders receive anything. Stockholders are entitled to their shares of the assets of the corporation only after all the creditors, of every kind, have been paid in full.

Bondholders, like other creditors, ordinarily, do not have the power to vote at any of the corporate meetings. Stockholders do have this right. In some instances, though rarely, the power to vote is given to bondholders, either by the terms of the mortgage or by the statute laws of the State.

The bondholders receive a fixed rate of interest on their bonds, which is a fixed charge or expense of the railroad company; the stockholders (of common stock) receive dividends on their stock dependent upon the condition of affairs of the company and as the board of directors shall declare them. The holder of the preferred stock is paid his stipulated rate of dividend only after the interest on the bonded indebtedness and all the annual fixed charges are paid. He is in the same position with relation to the bondholder as is the holder of the common stock, though his dividend is payable before that of the latter and sometimes his interest in the assets of the corporation has priority over that of the holder of common stock.

Bondholders are bound by the terms of the bond and mortgage; the contract between the parties.

The bondholder is bound by all the terms and provisions and conditions contained in his bond. He is chargeable with notice of all the facts that appear on its face or are endorsed on it. He is chargeable also with notice of all the terms, conditions, and provisions contained in the mortgage when the bond refers to the mortgage with sufficient directness to apprise him of its existence. The provisions of the mortgage, by such reference, become part of the bond with the same effect as if there set forth at length.

The bond and the mortgage constitute the contract between the bondholder, the railroad company, and the trustee. And like all contracts its provisions are binding on all the parties to it. It is in the construction that the courts put on the language used in these two documents, that the rights and remedies of the bondholders are to be found. The courts, in construing the language of the bond and the mortgage, are controlled by statute laws, the general precedents, and by the principles that apply particularly to railroad property and which govern the peculiar relations that exist between the bondholders and the trustee and the railroad company; all of which is read into and form part of the bond and mortgage. These statute laws, general precedents, and particular principles will be presented and discussed, throughout these pages, under the appropriate headings.

The legal residence of a railroad company is the State under the laws of which it is created; and it is the law of that State that governs the construction of the contract of the parties.

Each bondholder is bound by the terms of this contract; and each is entitled to its protection. And neither the trustee, nor any reorganization committee, nor any majority of the bond-holders, can deprive him of any of his rights by making any change in the terms of the bond or the mortgage, or by waiving any default by the railroad company under them, unless the bondholder has agreed and consented that they have such power. This power is to bind all the bondholders of an issue by the acts of a majority or of the trustee, may be conferred by the terms of the mortgage, or by the statute law of the States which, as was seen, forms part of the bond and the mortgage.

In case of a conflict between the terms of the bond and the mortgage, those of the bond will prevail; for the bond is the written evidence of the indebtedness, while the mortgage is the instrument merely that insures the payment of such indebtedness. The bond is the basic document: the mortgage depends on the bond for existence. There may be a bond without a mortgage; there cannot be a mortgage without a bond. Validity of bonds; over-issue; defective issue; issue in excess or abuse of power; issue in violation of law, or without power; secured by void mortgage.

Bonds issued by a railroad company in violation of its

charter, or the constitution of the State, or some of its statute laws, or issued without any power, are void.

Railroad bonds that are valid in the State in which the railroad company that issued them is incorporated, are valid everywhere. Where a road runs through two or more States, it must be incorporated under the laws of each. And should the bonds be valid under the laws of any of these States they are valid everywhere, even though they might have been invalid if issued under the laws of one or more of the other States in which the road is incorporated.

Bonds that are part of an over-issue or which have been defectively issued or which have been issued in excess or abuse of power where some power existed, are good in the hands of a bona fide holder, who has paid their reasonable value for them, purchased them in good faith before maturity, in the regular course of business, and without knowledge or notice of anything wrong. Should the holder of such bonds not meet all requirements of bona fide holdership, as just detailed, then such bonds are void in his hands. Over-issued or defectively issued bonds, or bonds issued in excess or in abuse of power where the railroad company had some power to make the issue, are good only in the hands of a bona fide holder.

But a distinction is drawn between bonds that are over-issued, or issued defectively, or in excess or in abuse of a power that it possessed, and those issued in violation of law or without any power at all to do so.

Bonds issued in violation of law or without any power are void in the hands of all holders, including bona fide holders. There is, in these latter cases, no mere error or abuse of power that the law will seek to cure when such bonds have come into the hands of innocent bona fide holders; but here is a violation of the law that the court cannot condone, and an absolute absence of power that the court cannot supply. However, where the railroad company has issued bonds without any power to do so, and it has actually received the money for them, the law will not permit it to benefit by its own wrong, and will then enforce payment of such bonds when held by bona fide holders. That is, notwithstanding that the railroad company had no power to issue the bonds in question, if it actually did, and received the money therefor, and they pass into the possession of holders who bought such bonds in good faith, before maturity in the regular course of business, and paid for them their reasonable value, and without knowledge or notice that anything was wrong, then the company must pay such bonds to holders answering all these requirements.

Bonds otherwise good are not affected by the fact that they are secured by a mortgage that is void or defective. Should the mortgage be void, for any reason, the security only fails and the bonds continue as theretofore. The bonds are good; the attempt to secure them has failed.

Many kinds of railroad bonds; classified generally as to form, security, purpose of issue, and mode of retirement, satisfaction, or exchange; distinctions pointed out.

There are many kinds of railroad bonds. The mortgages, too, that secure them vary in their terms.

It is doubtful if any two issues are exactly alike. However, they fall quite generally into classes that are basically similar, differing only with respect to some special agreement or stipulation.

The names used to designate issues of railroad bonds suggest, in a general way, these special agreement or stipulations that characterize an issue.

13—The entire railroad movement—seemed a complete failure. The Western Railroad, the Sacramento and Placerville line had fulfilled its mission. It only made short runs and serving as a means of commuting miners and their supplies back and forth to the "diggins." The farmers had turned to the fertile soils after they had robbed the streams of its gold.

"Enough of this life!"—moaned and groaned Mark Hopkins! From the beginning and in order to give some notion, and general opinion of what went on in the mind of Mr. Hopkins, at the existing time when the "Easterners" had failed in their financial backing to promote the Railroad Industry to a logical conclusion—Mark Hopkins decided that he should use his mint and mineral productions to promote Western Railroads to a superlative degree of success.

Mark Hopkins was born with a natural degree of aptitude and belief: "That faith was a candle in the dark, a fire that melted fear, undaring courage, fortitude, transformed doubt into doing, defeat into victory. He looked upon every task as one which could be surmounted with faith. Looked upon every task with strong, unswerving belief in a cause, an ideal —and most of all in one's self. In his opinionated world a situation was always viewed that no one could reach 'Fame's Hill' without these character constituents."

14—As an afterbirth—which has now grown into projects —which affect and effect the entire civilized world—including the economical structure of America and other Nations (which will be taken up with other books and encyclopedias in the future) Mark Hopkins made the decision to assume:

a. The responsibility of the "BOND SYSTEM" of the great RAILS—as heretofore referred to in the preceding paragraphs.

b. Leland Stanford, Charles Crocker, and Collis Potter Huntington were "STOCKHOLDERS" . . .

c. This was where the fraudulent schemes and conspiracy traps possessed and made its manifold attributes to the World's Number One "STEALTH."

d. Mark Hopkins was deprived of his *"Birthright!"* The lineage of Samuel Frederick Hopkins—who were a group of paupers—residing in St. Clair, Michigan, were used in lieu of the Heirs at Law of the railroad magnate.

e. The 1880 Federal Census enumeration shows that at the time Samuel Frederick Hopkins and his wife Mary Kellogg Hopkins were residing in St. Clair, Michigan and working in the household of John Rood—(who was running a cheap rooming house) and living in his household; but not a dollar of personal or real property reported for their board or recorded by the "GREAT AND MIGHTY FEDERAL LAND AGENTS, BANKERS AND FINANCIERS"—as being the "BROTHER" of the North Carolina Mark Hopkins—and who appeared on the scene and gave his affidavit before railroad attorneys—who affixed their notary seal as appearing in person to a conveyance of real property which conveyed title to a "Western Empire." See the "Instrument" of Samuel F. Hopkins and Moses Hopkins to Mary Frances Sherwood Hopkins, under date of Thirteenth day of March, in the year one thousand eight hundred and eighty (1880).

f. As a concrete and definite fact it can be proven by the United States Federal Census Record and other forms of documentation of equal value—that Samuel Frederick Hopkins never heard of the Railroad Magnate until the RAILROAD SCOUNDRELS, FEDERAL LAND AGENTS; AND HIS PAUPER "SONS" and the imposter wife of his brother, Mark Hopkins, of Lockport, New York, invited him in on the world's highest rated impostership.

g. NOTE: That on the date Samuel Frederick Hopkins appeared (March 13, 1880) in San Francisco before Charles F. Torbert, famous Notary Public and attorney in the overland chains of railroad in merger agreements of the subsidiaries. He and his wife Mary were living in the household with John Rood as above referred to.

h. The Federal enumeration under Schedule I—inhabitants of the United States Population Census Record was not enumerated until the nineteenth day of June 1880. This was almost a span of the time element of three months, after the purported document was signed by one of the nation's highest rated crooks upon which, Mr. Torbert affixed his notary seal.

i. Over two years had elapsed since the death of Mark Hopkins on March 29, 1878 until the document was signed March 13, 1880 and according to the residue of Samuel Frederick Hopkins it bears out my contention that: "He had never heard of the railroad magnate" and his "Signature," and personal appearance in San Francisco was like everything else that ever pertained to the adjudification of the North Carolina Mark Hopkins estate, was an act of forgery and impostership unheard of in American History.

j. Yet this deed of conveyance of the real property of Mark Hopkins was the instrument (deed) which passed title to the great Federal land grants and patents with a radius of:—"Twenty to thirty miles"—on each side of the "track clearance" of which Mark Hopkins retired under the bond system as described in the preceding paragraphs. It also conveyed title to the downtown site of San Francisco, the Mark Hopkins Hotel, the University of California, many townsites and cities, and other real properties too numerous to mention in a one volume book.

k. Is it any wonder that the author of this book, feels so strongly as her sentiments have proven by her years of dedication in unraveling the fraudulent scheme which took over the "Mark Hopkins Empire"—and of which not a one of his true and lawful "Heirs" ever received a red cent from the distribution of his estate.

l. But, what is another greater "Poison Pill" to swallow is evinced by the manner in which Mark Hopkins was murdered, unidentified, unknown, and unclaimed. And the group of the "IMPOSTERS" living in luxury, power, and fame who conveyed all real properties of which he died, seized and possessed and conveyed title under blood kinship by the impostership herein referred to.

m. The group of heirs of Mark Hopkins in North Carolina as a whole are poor and struggling to make an honorable livelihood, through the sweat of their brow. However, the progenitors came from generals, colonels, and statesmen from all ranks of life which built America. The Nation in which we all "Live, Move, and Have Our Being!" (Biblical quote.)

n. Even the greatest scoundrel and crook who ever sat in a "President Seat," or, the lowest person who ever died on death's row, would have to admit that the "Heirs At Law" deserve a better "fate than was handed down to them under the terms and conditions stated" and documented; to bear out every contention referred to in "CONTROVERSIAL MARK HOPKINS." (The revised edition has supplied quite a lot of additional evidence by the help of historian, history professors, national and state archivists, men and women of eminence and prominence throughout the United States. Or even abroad.)

William Alroid
 To
C. P. Huntington   Deed
Mark Hopkins &
Leland Stanford

Dated: July 20, 1871.

Consideration $166,400.00

Description of Property: All of the following described premises property, Franchises & effects to wit: All of the Railroad formerly owned & claimed & constructed by the Placerville & Sacramento Valley Railroad Co., located between the town of Folsom in the County of Sacramento, & the City of Placerville, in the County of El Dorado, all in the State of Calif. & constructed from Folsom to the town of Shingle Springs being the same Railroad, commonly known & called the Placerville & Sacramento Valley Railroad, also the franchises of the Corporations, the Placerville & Sacramento Valley Railroad Co. to construct, complete, maintain & operate said Railroad now built & hereafter to be built as fully & amply as said Placeville & Sacramento Valley Railroad Co. corporation might or could lawfully do & the right to collect tolls or payments for freight, passengers or other property on said Railroad, constructed or to be constructed also the right of way & land occupation for said Railroad now acquired & the superstructure of said Railroad now constructed or to be constructed under the corporate franchise of said Corporation, including therewith the road bed, iron ties, chains, spikes, bridges, culverts, aqueducts, turntables, fences & appurtenances of any nature name manner & kind, real & personal movable & unmovable in any way belonging thereto, also all the depots, watering places, stations, buildings & constructions of every nature fixed or unfixed to said Railroad belonging, also all offices & furniture, therein & materials of every nature & kind now on hand for the use of or belonging to said Railroad or Railroad Company, Also all the land, tenements hereditaments now granted or to be granted hereafter by the United States, or State or Corporation or person whomsoever to said Placerville & Sacramento Valley Railroad Co., or to any person for the use & benefit of said Railroad Co. as now built or as it may be hereafter constructed when fully completed & generally all real & personal property appurtaining to said Railroad of every nature & kind franchises rights & privileges, grants, donations, now belonging or which of right ought to belong or may hereafter at any time belong to said Placerville or Sacramento Valley Railroad Co., or any person for its use or benefit, together with all the estate of every manner or nature legal or equitable or mixed, with all & singular the tenements hereditaments & appurtenances, privileges, rights, immunities and franchises owned or claimed by the said Placerville & Sacramento Valley Railroad Co, & purchased by me under a judgment & decree of the District Court of the 11th Judicial District in and for the County of El Dorado in the suit of Wells Fargo & Co., Chas. E. McLane, Louis McLane & Danforthe N. Barney, Trustees, under the deed of trust bearing date Mar. 14th 1864 & such other deeds of trust as were used as evidence in said suit, as fully & completely as the same has been or shall hereafter be conveyed to me by the sheriff El Dorado County aforesaid, or by any Commissioner hereafter to be appointed by said Court for that purpose, and no other or greater right or title than has been or shall be thus conveyed.

Together with all & singular the tenements hereditaments & appurtenances thereunto belonging or in any wise appertaining & the revision & revisions, remainder & remainders, rents, issues & profits thereof & all the estate, right, title, claim interest, franchises & corporate rights, property possession, claim & demand whatsoever as will in law as in equity of the said party of the first part, of in or to the said premises & every part & parcel thereof, with the appurtenances.

William Alroid   (Seal)

Valley inserted before signing in the several places, also the words appertaining to said Railroad. Witness Robert Robinson, John H. Sanders.

Acknowledged July 27, 1871 J. Douglas Saunders, Notary Public.

Recorded Aug. 4, 1871. At 1035 A. M.

Recorded in Book 63. of Deeds Page 8. Sacramento County, Sacramento, Calif.

COPY OF THE DEED OF CONVEYANCE BY THE IMPOSTERS—SAMUEL F. HOPKINS AND MOSES HOPKINS

Samuel F. Hopkins
  and
Moses Hopkins
  to
Mary Frances Sherwood Hopkins

    This Indenture made the Thirteenth day of March in the year of our Lord one thousand eight hundred and Eighty Between Samuel F. Hopkins and Moses Hopkins heirs at law of Mark Hopkins deceased, parties of the first part and Mary Frances Sherwood Hopkins of the City and County of San Francisco, State of California the party of the second part. Witnesseth, that the said parties of the first part for and in consideration of the sum of One Dollar lawful money of the United States of America to them in hand paid by the said party of the second part, the receipt whereof is hereby acknowledged, do by these presents, grant bargain sell and convey, unto the said party of the second part and to her heirs and assigns forever, all of their right title and interest to and in all real estate of which the said Mark Hopkins died seized and possessed, situated, lying and being within the State of California: The interest of each of said parties of the first part in said real estate being one undivided eighth part which they hereby severally convey to the said party of the second part.

    Together with all and singular the tenements hereditaments and appurtenances thereunto belonging or in anywise appertaining, and the reversion and reversions, remainder and remainders, rents issues and profits thereof.

To have and to hold, all and singular the said premises, together with the appurtenances, unto the said party of the second part, her heirs and assigns forever.

In witness whereof, the said parties of the first part have here unto set their hands and seals the day and year first above written

Signed, Sealed and delivered in	Samuel F. Hopkins
presence of	(seal)
State of California	Moses Hopkins
City and County of San Francisco	(seal)

On this Thirteenth (13th) day of March in the year one thousand eight hundred and eighty (1880) before me, Charles J. Torbert, a Notary Public in and for the said City and County of San Francisco, duly commissioned and sworn, personally appeared Samuel F. Hopkins known to me to be the person whose name is subscribed to the within instrument, and acknowledged to me that he executed the same In witness whereof, I have hereunto set my hand and affixed my official seal the day and year in this Certificate first above written.

Charles J. Torbert, Notary Public

(SEAL)

In for the City and County of San Francisco, State of California.

State of California
City and County of San Francisco

On this Seventeenth (17th) day of March in the year One Thousand eight hundred and eighty (1880) before me Charles J. Torbert a Notary Public in and for the City and County of of San Francisco duly commissioned and sworn personally appeared Moses Hopkins known to me to be the person whose name is subscribed to the within instrument and acknowledged to me that he executed the same.

In witness whereof. I have hereunto set my hand and affixed my official seal the day and year in this Certificate first above written

(SEAL)

> Charles J. Torbert, Notary Public
> in and for the City and County of
> San Francisco
> State of California

Filed for record at the request of Wells Fargo & Co March 20th A D 1880 at 8 oclock AM and duly recorded in Book "FF" of Deeds page 777 & 778 Placer County Records F. D. Adams Recorder.

Recorded at the request of W. F. & Co on the 23 day of March 1880 at 12 hours 20 minutes PM in Book 100 of Deeds page 131 Sacramento County Records W. E. Gerbes

Recorder by G. W. Jackson Depy. Filed and Recorded at the request of Jonas Marcuse Agt Wells Fargo & Co., April 19th 1880 at 5½ oclk PM in Book "P" of Deeds pps 49 50 & 51 Sutter County Records W. H. Lee Recorder

Recorded at request of Agent WF & Co, April 22nd 1880

at 15 minutes past 11 oclock AM in Book 28 of Deeds Pages 60 61 & 62 Yolo Co Records W. D. Holcom Recorder.

Recorded at request of Wells Fargo & Co April 27th 1880 at 56 min past 11 AM in Book 28 of Deeds page 87 Records of Napa Co Cal. N. L. Nielson Co Recorder by Henry Brown Jr, Deputy

Recorded at the request of Wells Fargo & Co May 1st AD 1880 at 30 min past 1 oclock PM in Liber 74 of Deeds page 161 Solano County Records F. P. Weinmann Co Recorded by F. Wm. Gabriel Deputy.

Recorded at request of Wells Fargo & Co in Book 56 of Deeds Page 214 et seq. May 8th 1880 at 17 min past 2 oclock PM Records of Santa Clara Co Cal. HN Stephens County Recorder.

Recorded at request of Wells Fargo & Co May 18th 1880 at 9 oclock AM in Liber 32 of Deeds at page 525 Records of San Mateo County H. Walker Recorder by W. H. Lipp Deputy.

Recorded at request of Wells Fargo & Co May 21st 1880 at 45 min past 9 oclock AM in Book 22 of Deeds page 357 San Bernardino County Records A. F. McKenney Co Recorder by S. M. Wall Deputy.

Recorded at request of Wells Fargo & Co May 24th 1880 at 30 min past 8 AM in Book R of Deeds page 42 et seq Records of Merced County E. J. Hamilton County Recorder.

Recorded at the request of Wells Fargo & Co May 28th 1880 at 44 minutes past 9 AM I Book of Deeds page 464 to

466 Tehama County Records C. H. Greene Recorder by W. C. Campbell Deputy.

Recorded at Request of Wells Fargo May 29 AD 1880 at 30 min past 10 oclock AM in Liber No 29 of Deeds Pages 430 & C Yuba Co Records S. O. Gunning County Recorder.

Recorded at request of Wells Fargo & Co June 5 AD 1880 at 10 min past 2 PM in Vol 38 of Deeds page 142 Records of Contra Costa County C. Ed Miller County Recorder.

Recorded in the office of the County Recorder of the County of San Mateo May 15th 1880 at 9 oclock AM in Liber 32 of Deeds page 525. H Walker County Recorder by W H Lipp Deputy Recorder

Recorded at the request of Wells Fargo & Co. June 21st AD 1880 at 30 min past 1 PM

MARK HOPKINS MAINTAINED THE POSITION AS BOND-HOLDER—PRES. CONTRACT AND FI-NANCE CO. AND TRUSTEE UNTIL HIS DECEASE.

C.P.R.R. Co.

to

Contract & Finance Co.

To all to whom these presents shall come!
The Central Pacific Railroad Company
a Corporation duly incorporated and organized
under the laws of the State of California, and Mark Hopkins (successor to Charles Crocker) and Silas W. Sanderson, both of the City of Sacramento and State of California. Trustees of all the lands of the said Central Pacific Railroad

In Witness Whereof, the said CONTRACT AND FINANCE COMPANY has hereunto caused these presents to be signed by its President and Secretary, and sealed with its corporate seal, the day and year first above written.

Mark Hopkins
President, C. & F. Co.

W. E. Brown
Secretary, C. & F. Co.

Registered signature of Mark Hopkins as President of the Contract and Finance Company.

Company lying in the State of California and Nevada, and the Territory of Utah which remained unsold on the first day of October A.D. 1870, send Greeting:

Whereas on the first day of October A.D. 1870, the said Central Pacific Railroad Company conveyed all the lands lying in the State of California and Nevada, and the Territory of Utah, then unsold, of which the lands hereinafter described were and are a part to the said Charles Crocker and Silas W. Sanderson to hold in trust as security for the payment of Ten Thousand Bonds for the sum of One Thousand Dollars each, dated on the first day of October, A.D. 1870, and payable twenty years from date with interest at the rate of six per cent per annum, made and issued by the said Central Pacific Railroad Company.

And whereas, said Deed of Trust among other matters, provided that the said Central Pacific Railroad Company should have the sole and exclusive control and management of said lands, with full power to make sales of the same upon such terms and conditions as might, from time to time be agreed upon between the said Railroad Company and the said Trustees: and that when such sales had been made and the purchase money fully paid, the paid Company and the said Trustees should unite in a conveyance in fee simple of the lands so sold to the purchases thereof, which conveyance should absolutely and forever release the lands so conveyed from any and all lien or incumbrance, for or on account of said Bonds, or any other debt or obligation of the said Railroad Company.

And thereas, on the 14th day of August 1871 Charles Crocker, one of said Trustees, being about to depart from the

State of California to be absent for an indefinite period, did resign his trust under said conveyance of the first of October 1870: and whereas, on the 13th day of August, 1871, the said Silas W. Sanderson, the remaining Trustee under said conveyance did pursuant to the terms of his trust nominate Mark Hopkins of the City of Sacramento and State of California, to fill the vacancy caused by the resignation of said Charles Crocker and whereas on the 21st day of August 1871, the Board of Directors of the said Central Pacific Railroad Company, pursuant to the terms of said trust, did ratify and approve said nomination and did appoint said Mark Hopkins to fill said vacancy:

And whereas, the said Railroad Company has sold the lands hereinafter described, pursuant to the foregoing conditions to the Contract and Finance Company for the sum of Four hundred ($400) Dollars, which sum has been by it fully paid to the said Mark Hopkins and Silas W. Sanderson. Trustees as aforesaid.

Now therefore, in consideration of the premises and the said sum of Four hundred ($400) Dollars the receipt whereof is hereby acknowledged, the said Central Pacific Railroad Company and the said Mark Hopkins and Silas W. Sanderson, Trustees as aforesaid, do grant bargain sell and convey to the said Contract and Finance Company and its successors and assigns the following described tract of land situate lying and being in the County of Placer and State of California to wit:

The North West quarter (N.W.¼) of Section No. Thirteen (13) in Township Thirteen (13) North of Range Five (5) East, Mount Diablo base and Meridian containing One hundred and Sixty (160) acres according to the United States surveys together with all the privileges and appurtenances thereunto appertaining and belonging. Excepting and reserving, however, for Railroad purpose a strip of land Four hundred feet wide, lying equally on each side of the track of the Railroad of said Company, or any branch Railroad now or hereafter constructed on said lands and the right to use all water needed for the operating and repairing of said Railroads: and subject also to the reservation and condition that the said purchaser its successors and assigns, shall erect and maintain good and sufficient fences on both sides of said strip or strips of land; and also reserving all claim of the United States to the same as mineral land.

To have and to hold the aforesaid premises to the said Contract and Finance Company its successors and assigns, to its and their use and behoof forever.

In Testimony Whereof the said Central Pacific Railroad Company has caused these presents to be signed by its President and Secretary, and sealed with its Corporate Seal: and the said Mark Hopkins and Silas W. Sanderson, Trustees, have subscribed their names and affixed their Seals this Seventh (7th) day of September A.D. 1871.

Leland Stanford Prest. C.P.R.R. Co.
E. H. Miller Jr. Sect. C.P.R.R. Co.
Mark Hopkins, Trustees
S. W. Sanderson

State of California ⎫
County of Sacramento ⎭

On this Seventh (7th) day of September A.D. one thousand eight hundred and seventy one (1871) personally appeared before me Charles J. Forbest a Notary Public in and for said County, Leland Stanford personally known to me to be the President and E. W. Miller Jr. personally known to me to be Secretary of the within named Central Pacific Railroad Company, and personally known to me to be the persons described in and who executed the foregoing instrument, as such officers of said Company, who severally acknowledged to me that they executed the same freely and voluntarily as the free act and deed of said Company, and for the uses and purposes therein mentioned. Also, at the same time and place personally appeared before me. Mark Hopkins and Silas W. Sanderson personally known to me to be the persons and Trustees described in, and who executed the foregoing instrument as such Trustees, who severally acknowledged to me that they executed the same freely and voluntarily, and for the uses and purposes therein mentioned.

In Witness Whereof I have hereunto set my hand and affixed my Official Seal the day and year in this Certificate first above written.

Charles J. Forbest Notary Public

Filed for Record at request of Wells Fargo and Company. September 9th A.D. 1871 at 30 minutes past 10 O'clock A.M.

C. C. Cros by Recorder
By Jas. W. Smith Deputy

Hamilton Manufacturing Co.

WOOD - Printers Furniture - STEEL

Two Rivers, Wis.

October 25, 1929

(Registered Mail)

Miss Audora Garoutte
Care California Section - State Library
Sacramento, California

Dear Miss Garoutte:

I am enclosing herewith copy of a letter I
have written to Mr. J. W. S. Butler of Butler, Van
Dyke & Desmond, Sacramento, and also the original
letter written by Mark Hopkins to my grandfather at
Lockport, New York in 1853.

I hope that this letter may become a part
of your early day historical collection, and I also
hope that you may find among your early day notes some
mention of my grandfather's activities during those
wonderful times -- 1848 to 1852.

In case you desire to write me, my address
after November 10 will be Hotel Vista del Arroyo,
Pasadena, California.

Yours sincerely

J. E. Hamilton

(Courtesy of the California State Library.)

True copy of an original letter from Mr. J. E. Hamilton the
grandson who introduced the letter written by Mark Hopkins of
Lockport, N. Y. under the date of September 30, 1853. The
letter which Mr. Hamilton wrote to Mr. Allen R. Ottley, California Section Librarian on October 25, 1929 became a part of
early day Historical Collection of the State of California.

(Courtesy of the California State Library.)

Note that Mr. Hamilton refers to the boyhood days of his grandfather, Mr. Hamilton and Lockport, N. Y. Mark Hopkins who knew each other in an intimate capacity. Mr. Hamilton later came back in person and gave the complete lineage of the Mark Hopkins family.

(Courtesy of the California State Library.)

True copy of an original letter from Lockport, N. Y. Mark Hopkins, husband of Mary Frances Sherwood Hopkins the purported widow of the Railroad Magnate. The signature of the Railroad Magnate and that on the letter herein displayed was

(Courtesy of the California State Library.)

adjudged by Francis LaTullipe in Judge Hoyt's court to bear no similarity to the handwriting of Railroad Magnate, Mark Hopkins of N. C.

Dating back to the time that Judge Longdon and his wife Dr. Henrietta F. Longdon came to investigate the Heirship in North Carolina—they were seeking the handwriting of various people from the school days of Mark Hopkins, son of Edward Hopkins and Hannah Crow Hopkins of North Carolina. They reported that they were successful in their attempts to produce through various channels true specimens of the handwriting of the "Railroad Magnate"

As the progression went on, the evidence disclosed that there were "Two Mark Hopkinses" in California during the early years of railroad construction and promotional growth of Industry in Sacramento.

1—Attorneys, ranging from the "East Coast" to the "West Coast" were invited in on the litigation to investigate the fraudulent scheme which took over "THE GREAT SWINDLE OF AMERICAN HISTORY, AND FALSIFIED THE BIOGRAPHY OF THE GREAT CAROLINIAN —MARK HOPKINS."

2—The litigation folded up—the matter was quelled. The reasons will be stated in many pages of American History at a later date.

3—Apparently every library and historian had been deprived of the great revelation of a signature—which would bear out the contention that there were two signatures existing to make the discrimination between the Northern Mark Hopkins, from Lockport, New York, and the Mark Hopkins from North Carolina. (But to no "Avail".)

(a) Until one day the miracle happened; Mr. J. E. Hamilton, from the Hamilton Manufacturing Company walked into the California History Department of Sacramento and said: "I want to leave a letter—which I have been informed is one long sought. Mark Hopkins from Lockport, New York, was my grandfather's boyhood chum. The letter is suffice to show the intimacy"—"I am leaving the letter—which will be a matter of record—from the genuine handwriting of Mark Hopkins of Lockport, New York. Please keep this letter as a matter of history for the true identification of Mark Hopkins who married Mary Frances Sherwood September 20, 1854." (See the copy of the letter of Mr. Hamilton and the copy of the original letter of Mark Hopkins from Lockport, New York.)

4—Various handwriting experts were called upon to verify the signatures of Mark Hopkins from Lockport, New York, and Mark Hopkins, the Railroad Magnate.

(a) The handwriting experts herein referred to would come into the office of my attorneys; throw the documents on the desks and say: "I Am Having Nothing Further To Do With This Investigation! After all is said and done, my job and career is at stake!"

(b) When the case of Judge Hoyt was called, Mr. La-Tullipe was called upon to testify and he—"by now is receiving his reward in Paradise." He passed away through a mysterious death reported shortly thereafter. The following is a report from the local papers which reported his death—and asserted his lifetime achievements in the handwriting field of study. (He was one of the Nation's best.)

HANDWRITING REPORT

Francis X. LaTullipe, Esquire—the man who brought science to the Police Department and helped solve many of San

Francisco's most famous murders over the last four decades is dead. He was the first college graduate to become a San Francisco policeman. Mr. LaTullipe, spent a lifetime perfecting the department's crime and photo laboratories on the top floor of the Hall of Justice.

Mr. LaTullipe became one of the nation's handwriting experts and was used as an expert witness in trials throughout California.

His talent trapped Alfred Cline, suspected of murdering eight of his wives and then forging their names to phony checks.

Mr. LaTullipe appeared for me as "HANDWRITING EXPERT WITNESS" in the Judge Hoyt court—of which I obtained a copy of the genuine signature of Mark Hopkins the famous railroad magnate. I also obtained—not only the signature but a complete letter bearing all the comparative features upon which a handwriting expert could use for a comparative handwriting analysis—and the following results were obtained:

1. Mr. LaTullipe started off with expert laboratory tests—comparing the signature of the letter of Mark Hopkins and bearing out the entire handwriting throughout the letter with the signature of the Great Railroad Magnate, Mark Hopkins from Randolph County, North Carolina.

2. One of the signatures among many others of paramount importance was the name of Mark Hopkins—registered with the Contract and Finance Company. The other of equal importance was the signature as it appeared on the merger of the "Southern Pacific Railroad Company"—in which Mark Hopkins, of North Carolina, owned and controlled with Le-

land Stanford the entire capital stock of the giant stocks of over one hundred sixty (160) "OVERLAND CHAINS" independent subsidiaries and dependent subsidiaries—which spanned the American Continent.

(a) "THERE WERE ONLY SIXTY-FIVE (65) SHARES OUT OF THE ONE HUNDRED THOU-SAND SIXTY-FIVE (100,065) SHARES—OWNED BY HUNTINGTON, CROCKER AND THEIR ASSO-CIATES." . . .

HISTORY OF PROGRESS

A BRIEF OUTLINE OF ADDITIONAL PROGRESS
OF PROMOTIONAL VALUES CONDUCTIVE TO
THE CAPTURE OF THE "STOLEN EMPIRE!"
-ACQUIRED-
BY THE GREAT CAROLINIAN—MARK HOPKINS.
(1814-1878)

The copyright for Controversial Mark Hopkins was released in 1953—by Greenberg Publisher, and simultaneously
in Toronto, Canada, by Ambassador Books, LTD.—

A REPORT FROM THE PUBLISHER REPORT-
ED: "YOUR BOOK RECEIVED 90% MORE AND
BETTER REVIEWS THAN ALL BOOKS PUB-
LISHED!"

SINCE WRITING CONTROVERSIAL MARK HOP-
KINS—MANY DISCOVERIES EXPLORATIVE, AND
COMPRISING A MAGNITUDE OF EXPLORA-
TIONS INTO THE "HIGH LANDS OF THE MIND"
—HAVE ENTERED INTO THE DIRECT EXPON-
ENT—AND THE EXPONENTIAL MIND OF HU-
MANITY—THUS MAKING GREAT ATTRIBUTES
TO UNCOVER THE NATION'S GREATEST
"FRAUD".

The JOURNEY INTO THE HIGHLANDS OF THE HISTORICAL AND RESEARCH WORK BY THE AUTHOR OF THIS BOOK—HAS DEFINITELY STRENGTHENED MY FAITH IN THE HUMAN RACE—BECAUSE OF THE MANNER IN WHICH, AND BY WHICH, HISTORIANS—MEN AND WOMEN FROM ALL WALKS OF LIFE—HOLDING POSITIONS OF THE HIGHEST RANK, POSITION OR ATTAINING, STATION IN LIFE, RANGING, AND GOING BACK TO THE MOST HUMBLE WORKERS —MANY OF WHOM DID NOT ACQUIRE THE EDUCATIONAL ADVANTAGES OF THE EXECUTIVES AND OFFICIALS HEREIN REFERRED TO —BUT, HAD HIS HEART AND SOUL INTO HIS WORK, MADE A POINT OF JUSTICE A PARAMOUNT OBJECTIVE— THESE "SOLDIERS" representing honor "HAVE BEEN THE EMOTIONAL INSPIRATIONAL FLAMES THAT UNVEILED— MARK HOPKINS—THE GREAT CAROLINIAN— AND MADE IT POSSIBLE FOR HIM TO LIVE AGAIN!"

One is not AN EXTREMIST—FOREIGN FROM THE ORDINARY—OR IN ANY MANNER TRYING TO POSE AS THE EXCEEDINGLY GREAT— WHEN he can say with TRUE ASSURANCE—: "THAT A BAND OF ROGUES, MURDERS, THIEVES, AND CROOKS TOOK OVER TO AN EXTREMISM—AND, COLD-BLOODEDLY, AND DELIBERATELY STOLE AN EMPIRE OF WEALTH—LEFT BY THE GREAT PHILANTHROPIST — MARK   HOPKINS: — HIS

BLOOD RELATIONS—FROM THE NIECE AND NEPHEW LINEAGE OF DESCENT—NEVER RECEIVED A RED CENT!"

The treatment here-in-referred to is very deserving to the majority of the "HEIRS"—. The minority "GROUP"— have been the "SOLDIERS"—and the "COLLATERAL HEIRS"—which have comprised the "Financial Channels" in which one had to travel—along with the supplement of the "Soldier Heirs"—who, and, by whom—supplied the ways and means—which promoted the "Mark Hopkins, Stolen Empire"—to its present position!

The juridical reign of "jurisprudence"—tried desperately to establish into the minds of "THE HEIRS"—an adage: "A LOSS WHICH IS UNKNOWN IS NOT A LOSS!" (LATIN: "AMISSUM QUOD NESCITUR NON A MITTITUR")—WHICH IS A FAVORITE IN LEGAL VOCABULARY—WITH RESPECT TO THE Mark Hopkins millions—running into billions.

The reference here by referred to seems to have been a definite and deliberate one—: "There is in existence and has been since the date of the death of Mark Hopkins— March 29, 1878—every fraudulent act known to American History to take over the magnitude of wealth—which made The United States of America—become a rich and powerful NATION"—. This is evinced by the monopolic control that Mark Hopkins held in the "MINT PRODUCTIONS" —in San Francisco, Philadelphia, Denver, Colorado and other places of less prominence: "However, there was a complete loss of a report for a period of over thirty years in gold and silver!"

There is a skip in the chain of "TITLES FOR REAL PROPERTIES" for at least that span of time: "The earthquake in San Francisco is a great alibi!"—However, there was nothing destroyed in the earthquake of 1906—but, what could have been restored shortly thereafter—which would have and could have supplied every minute detail of legal descriptions.

The downtown site of San Francisco was located in Washington, D. C.

One often asks the question: "Where was it located?"

It is difficult for the mind to comprehend the fact that: "These treasured documents—upon which the Wells-Fargo Bank and Union Trust Co.—Crocker-Anglo Bank—MARK HOPKINS HOTEL, PALACE HOTEL, EVERY IMPORTANT HOTEL AND OFFICE BUILDING IN SAN FRANCISCO—THE UNITED STATES POST OFFICE, ET CETERA, ET CETERA, WERE FOUND IN THE RECORDS WITH AN AGRICULTURAL DEPARTMENT!"

"TITLE WAS VESTED IN THE NAME OF MARK HOPKINS UPON THE DATE OF HIS DEATH!"—

YET! San Francisco claims that "they were destroyed in the earthquake in 1906!"—

There will be a forthcoming "BOOK"—in the near future—that will be dynamite in itself—because "OF THE MANIFOLD DISCOVERIES AND ADDITIONAL INFORMATION—ILLUSTRATED BY ACTUAL DOCUMENTS—CERTIFIED BY CUSTODIANS OF RECORDS—RANGING FROM THE NATIONAL ARCHIVES OF THE UNITED STATES, STATE AR-

CHIVES, DEPARTMENT OF JUSTICE, AND EVERY FORM OF LOCAL, CITY, AND NATIONAL GOVERNMENT AGENCIES—OF ALL CATE GORIES!"

It is enough to say at this time: That this "BOOK" which will be published in the near future will prove that works of Bancroft referred to as: "THE UNIQUE COL- LECTION OF AMERICANA!"—WAS A GREAT FAKE OF HISTORY—DESIGNED TO ERASE THE GREAT CAROLINIAN—MARK HOPKINS FROM THE FACE OF AMERICAN HISTORY. NOT, ONLY, DID BANCROFT IN HIS WORKS FALSIFY THE BIOGRAPHY OF MARK HOPKINS BEYOND ALL FORMS OF RECOGNITION—BUT, EVERY HISTORIAN OF RECORD—REIGNING INTO OUR CONTEMPORANEOUS EXISTENCE: EITHER THAT or were guilty of a similar "cover up deal!"

"Honorable Historians" knew the falsifications, and were fully aware of the existence of what constituted, propelled the motivated deeds and acts behind the cold-blooded walls of injustice—"AND, REFUSED TO WRITE ANY- THING!"—Knowing, and being fully aware of the fact that anything one could ever say would have to be in error— because of the manner in which the great philanthropist's life had been falsified.

Due to popular demand—and request coming in daily for a copy of "Controversial Mark Hopkins"—it would be a great injustice for seekers of truth to be deprived of the privilege of having an autographed copy of the book.

Through a "FOUNDATION"—which is hereby "LISTED"—and the purposes for which it was founded—will enable Historical and Research Work to progress by leaps and bounds—thus enabling the part of "Historical Data" hitherto unknown to students—ranging from "HIGH SCHOOL DAYS THROUGHOUT ALL FORMS OF COLLEGE DEGREES!"—IT WILL OPEN A NEW WORLD TO HISTORIANS: ALL OF WHOM TELL THE AUTHOR OF CONTROVERSIAL MARK HOPKINS—"WE WANT HISTORY OF A VALUE AND QUALITY THAT WILL STAND THE TEST OF SOMETHING REAL AND ACTUAL, VERACITY, A TRUTH THAT IS IN ACCORD WITH FACT AND ACTUALITY!"

I am giving a quote from "THE COTHRAN HISTORICAL AND RESEARCH FOUNDATION"—

COTHRAN HISTORICAL AND RESEARCH FOUNDATION

An Organization designed to promote the Culture, Welfare, Happiness and Contentment of Humanity; and the *Sanity* of Mankind.

The COTHRAN HISTORICAL AND RESEARCH FOUNDATION has a tremendous purpose and its program will be dedicated to the practical application of the idealistic principles of Welfare and Happiness for the *"Most"* people. This program embraces the Positive and Constructive Action necessary for the accomplishment of actual and definite works of value to mankind.

The Foundation is chartered as a non-profit organization for altruistic purposes. It will disseminate literature and sponsor lectures to spread the doctrines of *"Constructivism"* —*"Purposeful Action For And By Humanity."* It will be a Research Center for all human beings seeking knowledge and the way to a fuller life.

PURPOSES & OBJECTIVES: To raise the morale of the American people. To prevent discontent from developing into social upheavel and revolution. To maintain Libraries for the dissemination of Historical and Psychoanalytic Literature of all Countries. To make useful citizens out of discontented, misunderstanding and misunderstood humanity. To maintain lecture halls where trained psychologists can instruct married groups, with special emphasis on mal-adjusted households where children are exposed to abnormal emotional environments. To conduct Historical Research and to disseminate such information through publications and to Sponsor Scholarships in the Handicrafts, Music and Literature, and in providing lectureships in Colleges and Universities. To establish Educational Institutions. To sponsor Boys and Girls clubs for the purpose of minimizing delinquency. To advance the cause of Justice in Democracy; sponsor Hospitals and the advancement of Medical Science.

To engage in any *"activities"* necessary or proper for the *"attainment"* of the *"chartered purposes"* for which this *"corporation"* is formed.

NO PART of the earnings or net income of the corporation may inure to the benefit of any member of the corporation, or any other private individual or party.

Since the Foundation is a non-profit nation-wide community service institution, the *"GIFTS"* made to it are *"deductible"* for both State and Federal tax purposes.

The COTHRAN HISTORICAL AND RESEARCH FOUNDATION seeks to spread the doctrine that IGNORANCE is the GREATEST SIN—and conversely—that KNOWLEDGE is POWER, STRENGTH, and of IMMEASURABLE, INFINITE, VIRTUE.

> COTHRAN HISTORICAL and
> RESEARCH FOUNDATION
> 1924 "K" Street,
> SACRAMENTO 14, California
> Duke University,
> Durham, North Carolina.

CONCLUSION

A great Historical Revelation will continue in force until the true "STORY" of the "STOLEN EMPIRE" of Mark Hopkins is brought into sublimation, and the nobility of his character is brought into the recognization it deserves on the pages of history.

The "STORY OF THE IMPOSTER OF THE SAM-UEL FREDERICK LINEAGE—AND, MARY FRAN-CES SHERWOOD HOPKINS—WIFE OF NEW YORK MARK HOPKINS WILL ALSO—BE TOLD AND DOCUMENTED BY FACTUAL DATA—WHICH WILL SUBSTANTIATE, SUPPORT, AND BEAR OUT EVERY CONTENTION!"

FURTHERMORE—AND, WHAT HAS PERHAPS BEEN A PARAMOUNT OBJECTIVE—, THE TRUE BIOGRAPHY OF THE FAMOUS NORTH CARO-LINIAN, MARK HOPKINS WILL BE RECOGNIZED THROUGHOUT THE NATION—IN EVERY LI-BRARY, SCHOOL, COLLEGE, CITY, COUNTY, STATE AND NATIONAL RESEARCH DEPART-MENT.

ANOTHER POINT OR PERHAPS A MORE AS-TOUNDING ACHIEVEMENT IS:

"THE STOLEN EMPIRE OF MARK HOPKINS WILL BE ORDERED FOR REDISTRIBUTION!"

END.

BIBLIOGRAPHY

In addition to Land Office, U. S. Census, and California and North Carolina Court records, newspaper accounts, city directors, deed books, and other documentary material, the following books were used for reference:

BANCROFT, HUBERT HOWE. *Chronicles of the Builders of the Commonwealth*, vol. V, VI, VII. San Francisco: The History Company, 1892.

CLELAND, ROBERT GLASS. *A History of California: The American Period.* New York: Macmillan Company, 1922.

CROFUTT. *Crofutt's New Overland Tourist*, vol. 1. Chicago: The Overland Publishing Co., 1878.

DAGGETT, STUART. *Chapters on the History of the Southern Pacific.* New York: Ronald Press Company, 1922.

FAULKNER, HAROLD UNDERWOOD. *American Economic History*, 6th edition. New York: Harper & Brothers, 1949.

FEDERAL WRITER'S PROJECT, CALIFORNIA. *California: A Guide to the Golden State.* New York: Hastings House, 1939.

GLASSCOCK, G. B. *A Golden Highway.* Indianapolis: Bobbs-Merrill Company, 1934.

HUNT, ROCKWELL D. AND SANCHEZ, NELLIE VAN DE GRIFT,

A Short History of California. New York: Thomas Y. Crowell, 1929.

LEWIS, OSCAR. *The Big Four.* New York: Alfred A. Knopf, 1938.

MORSE, JOHN FREDERICK. *The First History of Sacramento City.* Reprinted from 1853 edition by Sacramento Book Collector's Club, Sacramento: 1945.

PACIFIC RAILWAY COMMISSION. Report. Washington: Government Printing Office, 1887.

REDDING, B. B. *A Sketch of the Life of Mark Hopkins of California.* San Francisco: A. L. Bancroft & Company, 1881.

RIEGEL, ROBERT E. *America Moves West,* revised edition. New York: Henry Holt and Co., 1947.

SABIN, EDWIN L. *Building the Pacific Railway.* Philadelphia: J. B. Lippincott Company, 1919.

SHUCK, OSCAR T. *Representative and Leading Men of the Pacific.* San Francisco: Bacon & Company, 1870.

WHEAT, CARL I. "A Sketch of the Life of Theodore D. Judah." In *California Historical Society Quarterly,* vol. IV, No. 3.